ARRIVAL PRESS

POETS' PREMIERE

Edited

By

TIM SHARP

First published in Great Britain in 1997 by
ARRIVAL PRESS
1 - 2 Wainman Road, Woodston,
Peterborough, PE2 7BU

HB ISBN 1 85786 494 8
SB ISBN 1 85786 489 1

Foreword

Poets' Premiere is an anthology of poetry from authors who have never taken that bold step of sending their treasured, often very personal poetry for publication.

Whilst editing entries for this collection I found that there is a lot of undiscovered poetic talent still to be found.

I hope that after reading this collection you will agree with me that all the authors included fully deserve the recognition given.

All the poets in this book have joined forces to produce a truly wonderful collection of verse.

Tim Sharp
Editor

CONTENTS

GUESS WE'RE LOSING

Know what I would really love?
Peace on earth fit like a glove
See the inbred hate of fellow man
Disintegrate and be one clan
We'd have more to gain than lose
Could throw away our leather shoes
Let all creatures live their lives
Could throw away our guns and knives

Can't see it ever happening
When the world we live in is free from sin
Human nature's not that way
Help others but it has to pay

We're taught there's nothing wrong with greed
Having things that we don't need
Are the young the ones to blame?
Our ancestors taught us the game

We can't help our planet's fate
We must breed out our children's hate
Against colour against creed
Rid the violence rid the greed
The world would be a better place
Could be as one the human race

War on want I guess we're losing
When our own welfare is what we're choosing
Or maybe we have already lost
Promote ourselves at any cost
What are we doing to this earth
It's like abortion after birth

Ian Timpson

IT'S A GREAT LIFE

I sleep all day
I roam all night
I also get into
The occasional fight
I chase the birds
And get into strife
I fully intend
To enjoy my life
I bring mum presents
But she's never glad
She just scolds me
And says I'm bad
But I can get round her
I know how
I snuggle up on her lap
And give her my best
'Me-ow'

Margaret Randall

GOING HOME

You can never go back, a friend once said
To the streets where you used to tread
The thoughts and feelings are never the same
You will never be happy there again

Yet here I am. The train draws near
I'm filled with dread, trepidation, fear
Family commitments bring me back
My heart echoing the wheels on the track.

Reluctant I arrive at last
Haunted by the distant past
Chances missed. Mistakes I made
People I loved and then betrayed

Now duty done I leave once more
Return home to my sunny shore
To a new life, new dawn
Away from the place where I was born

Hazel Pullen

FOR YOU

I hear you scream from below
Shouting out to let you go
I only wish that I could help
But it's not that easy and you know . . .

Every day you send out your SOS
Please free me from this mess
To help would be to interfere
So I don't dare come near . . .

It's sad to be this way
But what more can I say
I might help another day
But like everyone else, I stay away . . .

To walk on by is an easier thing to do
I wish you knew how I feel for you
But I never see you, I don't know you
So I really don't know what to do . . .

So I sit and listen to your cry
As the time on my clock ticks by
So when you cry, I cry too
So I dedicate this poem to you.

Tracey Seivwright

JUST PASSING THROUGH

We first met when I was young
So bright and so naive
A stranger to the lonely world
I thought he would never leave.

But then one day he vanished
And was never to be seen
My heart forever searching
How could he be so mean?

I always wanted someone
To love me just for me
But he took away my innocence
So blind I could not see.

I thought I was in heaven
He made me feel so pure
But he did not really love me
I know that now for sure.

I gave him all my love
All my honesty and trust
But what I felt it was not love
It was just only lust.

Now I know love's just an illusion
It can tear your world apart
It deceives you and then leaves you
Until all that's left is an empty heart.

Kamini Tailor

CHILDHOOD

A childhood is a precious gift,
that should be happily remembered,
and sometimes missed.
Drawn upon when strength is needed,
Lessons learned, and wisdom heeded,
But when a childhood is bad,
and memories are only sad,
Strength is never there when needed,
Lessons never learned . . . and wisdom?
Well, that is only gained
through the pain and grief of a child
that needed . . .
the warmth and security of those
early days,
and above all his parents' *love* and *praise.*

Rae Piddington

SEASON IS THE BEST POET

Season is the best poet,
It knows how to write of springtime blooms,
And a million daffodils.
It knows how to write of soft summer sand,
And ice-creams on the beach.
It knows how to write of winter chill,
And the falling of the snow.
But best of all it knows,
How to write of autumn sunset,
And falling leaves that seem to glow.

Sophie Irvine

FUCHSIA

By the wisp of a thread,
hang the lanterns of red,
in a bed,
of colour and grace.

The blooms of the fuchsia,
seduce a bee passing,
and flashing,
it leaves without trace.

Abundant the droplets drip,
petals portraying
bells in profusion
silenced from playing.

Sudden breeze,
blows a sneeze
and causes the bells to unfreeze
their stillness and ring.

But still there's no chime,
they silently mime,
in time with each other they swing.

R A O'Donnell

LOVE?

Love love, oh what is this thing?
Could it be real, or is it just a dream?
Maybe it's real, but how can that be?
But with or without you right here by my side
I'm not quite sure how my feelings would lie!

How can a person mean so much?
When really you just wish you could hate their guts?

Dreamy thoughts as well as appetite loss and not
to mention the sleeplessness aren't really that bad.
But when your heart aches from being apart
And your insides and legs feel like jelly,
You know that you're not just being silly
This is real love with no denying!

Susan Campbell

THE SNOWDROP

This is the flower that greets the dawn
After the winter, when nature's reborn.
The little green shoots in the ground so bare
When there is still a chill,
In the cold night air.
The flower from the leaf so crisp and white,
Is so fresh to look at
In the clear daylight.
We know that spring is not far away,
When we look at the gardens
With their white bouquets.
There is something becoming
So pure and clean.
As I gaze with admiration,
Through the sun's bright sheen.
This is why, whether anyone else
Likes them or not.
'My favourite flower
Is the white snowdrop.'

Esther Sandford

ON HIS KNEES A MAN BY A BED

'Why?' Is the word that is always said.
'Why?' Is the thought that is in his head.
Held tight in his palm a picture of a child;
With a painted smile, and a soul pure and mild.

On his knees a man by a bed.
Staring at the pillow that once held a young head.
With tears they are thought; two words: 'Why part?'
Picture still in hand. Memory still in heart.

As clear as day were the sights in his mind.
The child's glowing eyes and a nature just as kind.
The sound of a voice that once filled a room.
The sound of a voice that was gone far too soon.

Nothing was asked nothing was gained;
Just acceptance and sorrow was all that remained.
From the moment of birth to the few years past;
A young child laugh that never would last.

He bowed down his head, cupped his hands in his face.
The tears rolled down dignity without trace.
On his knees a man by a bed.
A heart once full of love but now always bled.

When leaving the room his heart stayed behind.
With the same hurtful thoughts still locked in his mind:
'Why?' Is the word that always is said.
'Why?' Is the thought that is in his head.

Dean Smith

ALWAYS TOMORROW

I guess it took a little time for me to see,
The reason I was born into this world,
And what I'd have to go through,
For I've finally realised that I could be,
Better than before, definitely stronger,
I'll face whatever comes my way,
Savour each moment of the day,
Love as many people along the way,
Help someone who's giving up,
Even if it's just to raise my eyes and pray,
I've been alone inside myself for far too long,
I never really wanted it that way,
But I let it happen,
If I could do it all again,
My life would be,
Infinitely better than before,
I wouldn't waste a moment,
I'd make time for laughing with my friends,
Make music, make love, make amends,
Try to make a difference, try to love, try to understand,
Instead of just giving up, I'd use the power at my command,
'Cause there's always tomorrow to start again,
Before your last setting sun,
And everything your heart has longed for,
Has yet to be one,
Yes there's always tomorrow,
Though people come and they go,
But if you've brought some love into their lives
Then you've got something to show.

Karen Brent

OAK

Silent and still, empty of will
Oaken, tall and proud
Huge and strong, alone among
Sun and moon and cloud
In the clearing, always hearing
The muffles of mortal man
Rooted in splendour, devoid of gender
Knotted eyes that scan
The shallow reasons, changed only by seasons
Summer, autumn, spring
But what of the winter, and the snow that will linger
A white crown to make thee king
Of that wasteland still, oh what could fill
That wooden, xyloid heart
For free am I, yet I would die
Of thee to be part
To stand forever, alone together
Trapped amid the sod
Cleared of sin, we'd begin
And silent we'd wait for God

Kevin Curry

PALE DAWN

The landscape runs away from me,
Each hillside or peak becomes a fainter strip the further away it is.
All appear so sharp, yet it is as though they have been smothered,
In a warm blanket of mist.

Cotton candy clouds float around lazily at the break of day.
In colour they are muted,
Just whispers of pale pinks and blues.
But, a few of the undersides have been set alight by the rising sun,
Creating a strong dusty, red glow.

A lone shaft of sunlight strides up above the horizon,
Thrusting its warmth and light over the sober land below.

The infinite fiery orb is revealed, when the horizon dips
Down in shame at the night it has just given.
The sun soon forgives the semi-lit horizon and
Slowly but surely it rises, ever higher and stronger,
Casting the kind light of day down upon my lonely world.

Ross Ingham

MY FIRST DAY AT HIGH SCHOOL

Ties, trousers, shirts the lot
Not like the sixth formers, the scruffy lot,
Feeling hot and stuffy in your sweater
But at least it looks much better,
I walk into the doorway of the new school
Boys who walk past think they're really cool,
The other pupils all tower above
The sixth formers are all in love,
Everyone has to squeeze and push
Because it's always a mad rush,
You go down the corridor
And at the bottom wait at your door,
When you go in you sit and wait
Until in comes Mr Thistlethwaite,
Then after register you'll go to your first class
When break time comes you sit down and chat,
At home time when it finally comes
You either walk or wait for mums,
But when you go home it's not much fun
Because homework is still to be done.

Kimberley Walker (11)

RAINY STREETS

Walking into town
Weight of a world on my mind
The emptiness of sounds
From a world so unkind
Read again the letter
That tells me how you feel
The pain that it delivers
Makes my reality unreal
Keep my head low
And break the puddles with my feet
Listen to the rain
Whisper on these rainy streets
The trees they cry their leaves
And pave my path with gold
They no longer hide the sunshine
For the year is growing old
You left in the springtime
The summer sun no longer warm
Left me with memories
Of you in these arms
At night I go to places
Where shiny people meet
But by closing time
I'll be lonely
On these rainy streets

Robert Vickers

THE BOOKSHELF

On an aged wooden frame with dark wooden shelves
Each bowed with the weight of learning
Stand a thousand experiences from ages past
Full of knowledge to the wise and discerning.
The glory and shame of wars won and lost
Songs of love and compassion
Sonnets, odes, poems and dirges
Each written to leave an impression
On man's soul of the vastness of wisdom.
Yet this enlightenment given on trust
Far from accomplishing the desire of hearts,
Rests undisturbed . . . and covered in dust.

Sheila Corbett

THE SEA

In every travel brochure the sea looks
clear and blue
Rushing onto the white sands
Where lovers before have walked hand in hand

Everything looks calm and peaceful
Yet the sea changes all the time
As calm as a pond one minute
then raging as if possessed the next
throwing itself up against rocks and engulfing
everything and everyone in its path
It shows no mercy
It has no heart
It will calm down in time, and rest as if it were
asleep
but who knows what secrets lie beneath,
the now calm, clear blue waters of the deep.

Tracey Brodie

STITCHES OF LIFE

When a child enters this world
His life is like a clean white canvas
Waiting for someone to add the threads
The threads of their life
The threads of many colours
Which add depth and meaning to his life
Each new stitch is a new step
A step along the canvas of life
Sometimes the stitches unravel
A slip on the path of life
Mistakes are there to teach
The lessons of life
The canvas must be stitched into life
The child may begin to add his own stitches
The threads are sometimes difficult to follow
Nobody said life would be easy
Follow the pattern of life
It's there to be found
You just have to look
As the child grows
So the canvas grows
New stitches each day of his life
When the child becomes a man
He may leave and take the canvas
It is now time to stitch alone
Until he meets someone to love
They will then stitch together
To complete the canvas
The canvas of life
With the stitches of their love

Julie Pitcher

I LOVE YOU STILL

It came like a bolt from the blue
I cannot believe this could happen to you
They could not reach anyone else that day
So your friend, phoned me, I still cared in every way
I dashed to your bedside, you were very still
I was told you were really sick, really ill
You called my name, over again
But nothing will ever be the same
All day, I sat by your side, my dear
Hoping, praying, thinking, all filled with fear
All the plans, we made are through
Though, I still love you true
Then you took my hand
The tears, and you were all I could stand
You spoke, for the very last time
The words, you were sure, were mine
Then you closed your eyes, and died
And I just sat there and cried
The nurse, came to take me away
Oh why, I ask, did it have to happen on our wedding day
Perhaps, I should have told them back there
That your girl, wasn't me, but I still care
That a few months ago, you broke my heart
But I never dreamt that this way we would really part.

Rosemary Cleaver

THAT SINKING HEART

Throughout our lives there'll always be
Someone special who we did see
In my heart all time stands still
A love so dear no one could kill

You'll never know how much I care
For me to say would be unfair
If someone bottled my feelings clear
Fortune awaits without a fear

With you my heart is full of joy
To get a 'yes', it was my ploy
'Til now perhaps I never knew
Just how love for you it grew

I'll miss you soon, that smiling face
Those lovely eyes without a trace
Of all the times so precious, so pure
For a lonely soul, what is the cure?

You're my best friend now and forever be
Never leave me sad or you will see
Just how much you really meant
From heaven's gate you were sent

For that sinking heart

Paul Davis

THE OCEAN

The waves of foam roll towards their journey's end.
Breathtakingly beautiful,
With such power, crescending in a show of might,
And then no more.
Just fingers reaching out to touch,
But never quite.

Peter Neeves

SNOW

Not a drop of snow in sight,
On that dark and cloudy night,
Until the white mass of snow lay down,
And covered our small and quiet town.

In a few hours the place was white,
Things were such a beautiful sight,
Children play with their sledges in the snow,
Yet older people dare not go.

Outside the trees were white and clear,
Of which some people may have a fear,
But this weather not long will last,
Then it will go into our past.

But make the most of its beauty now,
In whatever way you know how,
Its beauty is there for you and me,
And what you see is completely free.

Eileen Watson (15)

MY CURE FOR THE BLUES

For most of my life I've been happy.
But like everyone else there comes a time.
When I feel I can't cope.
I'm at the end of my rope.
There are too many mountains to climb.

When I'm down I try counting my blessings.
Of which I have quite a few.
But I must make it clear.
Sometimes this does not cheer.
And I don't always know what to do.

On occasions I get very angry,
And I let my temper flare.
I feel better then,
Than other times, when
I'm lethargic and really don't care.

I know there are lots of others.
Who are much worse off than me.
But they don't make me sad.
When I'm feeling bad.
I don't think misery loves company.

Now I find writing poetry helps me.
My thoughts and ideas to express.
I can write it all down,
And not feel like a clown.
Try it, when you are next under stress.

Elizabeth Wren

ACT OF GOD

Tempests may rage about your head
But let your heart be free
Release your cares, and all your woes
Just give them all to me.
For I will guide and comfort you
I'll be your stay and friend
Believe in me, my little one,
Now, and until the end.
Beloved child, I set you free
Now, serve me as you should
Don't let dark dread obscure your eyes
Be true, my child, to me.
Just trust the vision of your eyes
and let your heart be free.

Lily Knightley

LADY IN WHITE

A slender sheet of white,
Reflecting in the moonlit night,
Sighing a deep sigh,
She sings a lullaby.

Slender and tall she walks,
And with her lover she talks,
Their hearts beating as one,
And sweet music has just begun.

Their lips meet in a tender kiss,
And for moments they're in heavenly bliss,
Then they both ran into the distant light,
Her lover and the lady in white.

R T Shah

LAST SUPPER

An empty cup, a plate,
The scattered crumbs;
A common enough still-life from many rooms.
The clock is ticking softly. I am surprised that it does.
I never noticed it before, and now
Time has stopped for you.
Or has it?

The crumpled serviette had fallen to the floor
As you got up to take your customary rest.
In memory you are heavy now and slow,
Although I never noticed it before.

Two cushions are arranged against the seat,
Your library book is open, and your glasses placed
Lens down upon the page. I know immediately
You didn't put them there. I know how carefully you polished them
And placed them in the case before you went to sleep. And now . . .
An empty room, a page unfinished, the sun
Still shining in the leaded lights, a rainbow on the floor.
Beyond the garden gate life hurries on
Although I never heard it pass before.

And so I will no longer be your child. And this will be
No safe enchanted tower.
I close the book, brush off the crumbs,
Walk backwards from this strange familiar room.
Soon life will creep back in beneath the door,
Because this is an ordinary place
Although I never realised before.

Kath Barnard

ENGLAND

From the misty shore of the lake of Windermere,
To the craggy Cornwall cliffs of The Lizard,
Those dark-age tales of might, magic and fear,
Still ring true with King Arthur and his wizard.

Men fought through the ages, for the cross of St George,
Once in bright armour, then red coats, now in green and brown,
Enough blood has been spilled to fill the devil's gorge,
Just so the emperor can justify his thorny crown.

But as dawn breaks over England new,
A tired and weary land we now see,
No empire now, our outposts are few,
No tyrant to cause a bended knee.

Peace reigns once more, or can it still,
While through Europe's unity, ourselves we lose,
Our identity lost, we are crushed until,
We become numbers, no freedom left to cruise.

We look around, and see this corruption and decay,
Where money means everything, and nothing at all,
While my forefathers fought for all those things given away,
This country now the last piece of junk on the white elephant stall.

So to those who will come to power I beseech thee,
From the warrior with no weapon but a pen to resort,
Wield the power just and fair, don't lose our right to be free,
From the tyranny of those who oppress and are quick to retort.

And so to my birthland this last dying request,
Don't lose our forefathers' shame and glory,
We lost so much at someone else's behest,
And this will end my fair England's story!

K A J Ridgway

HOLIDAYS

The holidays are here once more
And it's nice to walk along the shore,
Taking time to stand and stare
At people sitting in deck chairs.
Some are reading, some are sleeping,
Some are eating ice-cream cones
Some are writing postcards home,
Telling their friends and relations
All about the jubilations
But at last the time has come,
For us to make the journey home.
Now there is just time to say,
Hope to come back another day.

V Giltrow

PEARL DIVING

Are you crushed like a pearl
enveloped yet not defeated?
Can you swim in the swirl
abandoned but not beneath it?
If you fly from your mould
are you threatened, are you cheated?
Do you crave for something new
even though you cannot reach it?
Should you leap beyond your bounds
knowing you'll come back broken hearted?
Or will you just lie still
and sleep and whisper and forget?

K E Sanders

THE CARAVAN

The holidays are coming round fast,
Where shall we stay - at the flat we had last?
Or an hotel, bed and breakfast, we think and we plan,
Then a bright idea dawns - we'll hire a caravan.

The children were thrilled when we arrived at the site,
How I wished I was able to share their delight,
For there as I looked - my face going stiff
Was our van - perched right on top of a cliff.

It was safe I was told, chained to the ground,
But what chains the ground, said I without sound,
Let's go in said the children, we want to explore,
I stepped in - crashed my head on an open cupboard door.

Next morning I rose after a very rocky night,
The fog horn was blowing with all of its might,
We needed some water, so I got me a pail,
Opened the door - to be blown out by a force 8 gale.

To go out was freezing, to stay in was worse,
Two children in a caravan are a positive curse,
And every now and then would come the frantic call -
Hey mum! It's that bed again, it's fallen from the wall.

At last it's all over, our cases we pack,
Let's hurry, let's go, I can't wait to get back,
Caravans are not for me, by now you must know,
Comfort's my thing - so next year it's a flat
But to all you brave caravaners - I take off my hat.

Irene Rice

JUST INSIDE

Have you got someone to talk to,
Who offers you wisdom and care,
Whose company ever excites you
and will cherish the minutes you share?

Have you got moments to treasure,
Memories filled, like a store?
So when you get older and bolder
You'll talk over them evermore.

Have you got comfort and laughter?
Joy like an endless stream,
and places, faces with smiles there,
so that life itself feels like a dream.

Have you got new adventures,
Mysteries open to you,
like a childlike expectancy, of thrills,
to carry you through?

Have you got this pearl, this rock,
this door - to which the key
to endless love, is sitting there
just inside you and me.

Amy Seed

WINTER OLYMPICS!

I would love to be in a bobsleigh race
A helmet and goggles upon my face

You'd hear the sled go *swish*
As down the hill I race

Or to be in the downhill ski jump
And go flying into space
To land upon my skis
And not upon my face

To be there with the champions
When I receive the gold
I would be a hero
As I'm only 8 years old

R N Tate

A BETTER PLACE

Why when there's sun, do I feel cold,
Why at this age, do I feel old,
Why am I feeble, when I was so bold,
Please help me find my soul.
The strength I had has all but gone,
So what have I been doing wrong,
Perhaps with the killing of an unborn son,
I sacrificed my soul.
All I long for is a happy life,
two kids, a house and beautiful wife,
but until I find some peace within,
the life I long for can't begin.
So should I end it all today,
just pull the trigger and drift away,
Maybe to a better place,
Where I feel the sun upon my face.

Kevin Young

UNTITLED

I'm going on a diet,
I know that's nothing new,
But where I had one spare tyre
I've now discovered two.

My bra is like a hammock,
Where it used to be petite,
When I let them out at night,
They're half way to my feet.

I've tried to shrink my stomach,
But afraid to no avail,
When I lay down in the bath,
I look just like a whale.

So I'll start my diet tomorrow,
and I want to get it right,
So I don't give in to temptation,
I'll eat these chocs tonight.

Jennifer Petty

THE COST

The fabled moon and the stars
You were to me -
The sound of the wind and the rain,
The light of the sun through bars -
Ultimate joy
And now only pain.
If you no longer love me,
Why don't you say?
I know the rule -
Take what you want from life -
Take it and pay.

M P S Denton

INNOCENCE

Through the infinity of nothing a consciousness grows,
From an immortal personality a mortality it now knows.
In the eternity of God a child now appears,
Finding the world with eyes, nose and ears.
Free from the cancerous corruptions of life,
Not seeing a society where immorality is rife.
An innocence leads to a love of all,
comforting images of allies so tall.
Rejoicing in the simplicity of shapes and colours,
Always relaxing in the safety of others.
Attempting to explore the complexity of the world,
Into a corporeal, viviparous puzzle it is hurled.
Trying to unravel the intricacies of communication,
To express yourself, and master interpretation.
Through the medium of joyful play the entity learns,
The standards of an expectant society it discerns.
Parents and relatives rejoice in the child,
Its purity special, its manner so mild.
The incarnation of trust and hope,
But in a modern philosophy, can it cope?
It must not trust, it cannot love,
To survive in a capitalistic 'push and shove',
The naïve attitude must be changed,
The child's mental reasoning is to be rearranged.
We have reverted, degenerating back,
The values of the young in adults we lack.
People become just the dust of which they're made,
Simply their shell, their soul decayed.
We must return to the eternity of love,
To have a child's heart - on the wings of a dove.

Charles Henn

BELIEVE

I sat on the wall,
looking out to sea.
Waiting for my call,
I know they need me.

The waves are crashing in,
like tree branches in the wind.
A view that's transfixed within,
a small piece of beauty is being thinned.

I leave this paradise,
and head back to reality.
I feel that at a price,
this utopia could be normality.

C B Wright

WONDER WHY

Blackbirds, swallows, birds are free
Not like you and me,
They fly in the sky
And I wonder why?
I can't fly.
Up up high they go
In wind, rain, or snow.
But they get wet
And I keep dry
That's why I can't fly.
So now I'm glad
And not just sad,
They are free
And I'm happy I'm me.

R Maskill

THE GREEN MEADOW

I see across the meadow green,
The gulls in flight - they dip and scream,
And hear the song - as soft I tread
Of gentler birds, above my head.

The trees give shade, I rest and doze,
Then wake - to find the twitching nose
Of a field mouse, raised up in the air,
Wondering what I'm doing there?

I watch - trying not to breathe at all,
Or move - though cramped - I do recall.
A sound disturbed the tiny mite,
Who disappeared in obvious fright.

A farmer, coming through the glade,
Saw me resting in the shade . .
Stopped to pass the time of day,
Before proceeding on his way . .

I quickly rose - in some alarm
Remembering the gun beneath his arm . .
I left that idyll in the sun,
Along the way the man had come.

Not keen to hear the harsh report,
Soon to come - for life seems naught.
Then all would know - that death had come.
Near to that meadow, in the sun.

Dennis A Stiff

WALK ABOUT

I wish I was clever and could
Write about
The beauty I see when I'm
Walking out
The trees in the winter all
Dressed in white
The crocus, the snowdrops a
Beautiful sight
The fields and the meadows
In summer it seems
Weave a beautiful blanket
For mother earth as she dreams
And see how the daffodils
They nod and they sway
And send out their greeting
'Have a wonderful day'
I wish I was clever and could
Write about
The beauty I see when I'm
Walking out

A Kyle

THE THINGS I SEE AND LIKE

Speed boats, surfboards
people in the sea, I walk along
the shore it inspires me,
every time I hear the waves
lap against the sand there are skimmed
pebbles from the land
In the harbour by the hill
I see the boats moored and still.

Gareth Evans (8)

ODE TO BABY SARAH

Oh! Sarah dear how precious
You have become to us.
That mop of hair,
Those sparkling eyes,
Your toes and fingers hypnotise.

A voice that was once just a squeak,
Like baby kittens calling,
Has learned to make a bill and coo,
At feed times even bawling.

We watch your progress every day
To see how you have grown
Amazed to see you taking note
As though this was unknown.

So if the thoughts do cross your mind
That grownups all seem funny,
Please try to make allowances
Especially for mummy.

The funny faces that she pulls,
That probing tickling finger
Are efforts for us to enjoy
Your cutest smiles that linger.

But remember this dear Sarah,
When you grow big and strong,
You can always get your own back
And tickle her all day long!

P Peck

THE GOLDFISH

Gold and lithe with moving tail
Lovely for the eye to see
Darting furtively about
Hoping that we'll set you free.
Send you to an island fair
And release you in a pool
Where weeds grow in abundance
And the water's clean and cool.

Oh little fish and can we tell
By your water symphony
Do your constrained movements
Show you're waiting patiently?
For some unknown future time
To come like the dawn of day
When you'll be so alert and free
To hunt and venture all the way,

Now you're swimming round and round
Aquatic memories are small
But faintly still your fish's mind
Responds to a greater call.
A call to swim in waters wide
Away from a goldfish bowl.
Oh little, lovely, golden fish
I hope you have a soul!

Thelma Paolozzi

YOUR VOICE

Your voice
skin-dives in me,
wearing the wet-suit of night.

It swims past
my anemone hands,
en route to the reef
of my spine.

Your voice
keeps that shark sleep
at bay,
as it starts
to circle.

It's high-tide:
your voice dives low,
prises my oyster open,
finds the pearl.

Your voice
is Jonah,
swallowed whole,
my womb
the whale.

Susan Richardson

POEM

To hold a word that
touches my thoughts
feels my heart
warms my breath.

To build a sentence that
will remain, in the
hearts of others, when
I can no longer see it.

To write a verse so full
of my own being
that it may be
recognised as well as
my reflection in the mirror.

To pen a few lines that
leap to life when
another's eyes touch the
page and absorb
my own self.

Katie Johnson

MY CHILDREN

Grubby hands and scraped brown knees
Tousled heads from garden play
Cheeks like roses - full of life
That was my children yesterday.

A bird on a tree - a wondrous sight
Raspberry bushes - a magic wood
Digging holes for treasures deep
No time to think of sleep or food

Where did they go - those precious years?
When life was full, and days sped by
Doctor, dentist, school events
A lot of laughter - a lot of play

Teenage tantrums came and went
Life beckoned - I knew they couldn't stay
Now, adults, showing love and care
That is my children of today

Margaret Ross

THE SHOEMAKER

His repair shop smells of leather,
Damp and musk in rainy weather;
Around the walls in wire cage -
Linnets sing of nature's rage.

Their love songs - never meant for him
Repairing shoes with soles so thin;
In warm April, when the linnet breeds,
They cry for insects and sweet flower seeds.

Incarcerated in his shop,
From wire to perch they tend to hop;
As he cobbles shoes from morn till night
His mouth so full of tingles bright.

He nails a sole - cut from bend of leather,
(While linnets sing of heath and heather)
Oblivious to the linnet's plea
Please, Mr Cobbler - set us free!

But, he taps away until old age;
And sweet linnets die in rusting cage.

R H Greedy

THE REFUGEE

Through misty eyes, what's that I see
A ship, a speck on a tranquil sea.
The slow approach how big it seems
The answer to so many dreams.
Pitiful faces, full of awe watch over the rails so close
to the shore.
They disembark, do they feel free?
Could this be the answer to their pitiful plea.
The soldiers stand with guns on show.
No welcome here, just get up and go.
The lorries move along the quay, their cargo's quiet,
no sounds of glee.
These people here, yes they know great pain.
No jobs, no homes, just human shame.
Their dreams and hopes of living free
Find this is the life of the refugee.
Always moved on, never welcome here
Their eyes are wide just full of fear.
Could someone here just give them hope
Maybe another bus, lorry or boat.
When will they find that special friend
God says 'my children come unto me'.
Does He know the plight of the refugee?
As daylight fades and sleep is near
God give them hope to quell their fears
God grant them peace with no more tears.

Lucille Woods

THE PEACE OF GOD

Where can we find that precious thing?
Church bells ring, children sing:
Where can we find the peace of God?
In grassy sod, or mountain high,
or trees that reach up to the sky?
Will we find it in a wistful smile
or find it in going the second mile?
We try and find it in our home,
unless despair doth make us roam.
We see it in those eyes so blue,
when a tender child looks up to you.
We hear it in the wood dove's coo,
and when a loved one comes in view.
Where can we find the peace of God?
Where *love* is, that's for sure:
The kind that will endure,
Through strain and stress and sore distress:
There we will find the peace of God.
And in a quiet, peaceful, home
Where lights burn low, wood fires blaze,
soup simmers, coffee bubbles, tea infuses
and smiles are kind and warm.
No strife, no bitterness to quench the embers.
A garden full of flowers and birds that sing.
And in the great hills, the peaceful lakes
the river's magic, the roar of the mighty oceans,
There will we find *God*, astride like a Colossus,
all petty feuds forgotten.
And in *silence* and fresh air, unpolluted
there will He reign.
But in a *kindly heart* He reigns *supreme*
and life becomes a pleasant dream.

P S Christie

HORSE SENSE

'It's just like riding a bike' she said,
'You mount up and off you go,
It hasn't got brakes or pedals,
But it's just the same, don't you know'
Her daughter looked at her scornfully,
And said 'You know nothing at all,
It's not much like riding a bike,
Especially when you fall'.
Her mother didn't believe her,
Her mother said 'Well I don't know'
She said 'Just get yourself dressed,
and then we'll be ready to go'
They went off and got it ready,
And brought it out into the yard,
It looked at them and thought 'neigh
I'll teach them a lesson that's hard.
I don't have brakes or pedals,
I don't have wheels that go round,
If it's just like riding a bike,
What's she doing down there on the ground?'

Carolyn Reed

THE WORLD AT WAR

Uncertainty, unsure and painfully unaware
Of how time passes us by and leaves us standing
Standing alone left only to stare
At a world that does not know where it is going

A world where mercy may never have a place
In the turmoil and the killing of the innocent
A land full of hatred, bigotry and war
Where the taking of a life can be imminent

Many people have tried to show an air of calm
To spread the word of peace through the bloodshed
Trying desperately to tell us just how wrong we are
To have feelings that show nothing more than hatred

Sharon Crawford

MY BRAVEHEART

This wounded heart of mine doth try,
To hide its ache from mine own eye.
This wounded heart of mine cries out,
On mine deaf ears it would shout.

I carry on without a show,
As big as life, so no one would know.
Torn apart my heart sings out,
Cleaved in two without a doubt.

To mask my sorrow I would say,
Heart of mine live for today.
Do not falter, do not fail,
Let your beat carry us down this trail.

Will it end my heart replies,
Will it end my heart's desires.
Will it cause me to reject,
To sit and ponder and reflect.

Let us heal this pain and sorrow,
It will lessen by tomorrow.
Life goes on for you and I,
On and on until we die: my braveheart.

D B Allan

FOR OLD TIME'S SAKE

The time has come for me to go
Back to the place that was my home,
To walk Brantfell, view the lake
Windermere for old time's sake.

See the sunrise, first of spring
Hear the birds when first they sing
See the trees that once were bare
Smell the blossom in the air.

Waving bracken on the fells
Hear the chimes from the old church bells,
Lambing season just beginning
Hear the sound of far-off bleating.

Gardeners busy with their spades
Turning soil so flowers won't fade,
In full bloom and patchwork still
Their fragrance drifts up to Brantfell.

Where I have sat in bygone days
to view the lake in childhood gaze,
Round the bandstand we use to scamper
Till the hour got dark and damper.

Above the fells the sun now setting
Our sound of laughter turned to fretting,
Back home to mum, supper and bed
Or would it be a scolding instead.

And now the lake lies calm and still
Moonlight shadows cloud Brantfell
The peace and calm of Bowness Bay
Lies still, waiting for another day
When I'll be back to view the lake
Windermere for old time's sake.

Bob Clayton

THUNDER STORM

Did you see that lightning
A searing flash of power
Straight down from the heavens
A storm was not a shower

Brilliant flash of yellow light
You see it then it's gone
Just for that split second
The thunder won't be long

You can hear it rumbling
And then it's overhead
Just the opposite to lightning
Can wake you from your bed

Lightning is the quiet one
So deadly this can be
Coming down forked lightning
Power to split a tree

Never hear a rumbling
Nothing, there is none
Just in that split second
Some damage can be done

So vivid when you see it
It really lights the sky
See it in the distance
And when it passes by

Many stories we hear tell
When lightning does appear
Listen to that thunder storm
Will very soon be here

L J Judd

THE INDOMITABLE SPIRIT

The spirit of this island
Will always be there,
A true British feeling
Of things that are fair.

To help when it's needed
Whatever the cost.
Champion the under-dog
Even when lost.

Don't let us lose this,
It matters too much.
Our history is glorious
With a true common touch.

Of people who care,
For things that are right.
So let's all pull together
And fight the good fight.

There is no better nation
On the face of this earth,
We don't need a re-tread,
Just a spiritual rebirth.

Noelle E Capes

SARAH'S SILVER POEM

A little silver princess
Lived in a silver house
She wore a silver locket
Of a little silver mouse.

The little silver princess
Sat upon a silver chair
And with a silver brush and comb
She combed her silver hair.

The little silver princess
Slept on a silver bed
And wrapped in a silver sheet
She would rest her sleepy head.

Sarah Jane Holland (8)

IN EVENING SHADES OF DOUBT

As I sit and watch the sunset
On another lonely day,
I miss you more than ever
More than mere words can ever say.

You gave me life you gave me love
You asked nothing in return,
You gave without conditions
A lesson I hope that I have learned.

Like all children I took you for granted,
Presumed you would always be there
But I lost you before I was ready,
God, why is life so damned unfair?

Oh how I wish I could tell you
Of the love that I felt inside
Of the happiness that you gave me
Of the feelings I was stupid to hide.

And because I was stupid and hid them,
Never letting those feelings of love out
I sit and wonder if you knew how I loved you
In these evening shades of doubt.

Alan Lowe

WINTER

I cannot wait for winter
It's my favourite time of year.
When I look out through the window
And see the snow appear.

To see it glistening all around
Is such a sight to see.
The children building snowmen
Before being called in for tea.

Then there's Christmas coming
Carol singers by the score,
With trees and decorations
And wreaths upon the door.

There are Christmas cards and holly
All around the room.
Christmas stockings hanging
For Santa's coming soon.

And then before you know it
We're giving a great big cheer.
For we are just beginning
A bright and *happy new year.*

K M Thorpe

ODE TO AN UNBORN CHILD

I didn't get to see you
I can never hear your cries
I don't know what sex you were
Or the colour of your eyes.

I can never see you smile
Nor hold you close to me
You would have been very special
But that wasn't meant to be.

So please forgive me little one
If sometimes I do cry
For I am your mummy
And I could not say goodbye!

Linda Scott

MUM - THE LOLLIPOP LADY

When mum came home, announced her new job
My first reaction was - *Oh my God!*
A yellow hat and gloves too
Bright, shiny, colourful, new,
To help the kids, she had the heart.
She had the gear, ready to start.
Stopping cars at forty miles per hour!
A tremendous deed, mum didn't cower.
She is courageous! Stopping cars dead.
With that fluorescent hat on her head!
At Christmas all the children were grateful,
Even the cars will not feel hateful!
Chocolates and cards cluttered up,
Being petted like a pup!
The Quality Street piled in,
To mock this woman is a sin!
We now, all approve of her new career,
Although it's full of danger and of fear.
We must commend her new pastime,
The amazing deeds of her job; are in
this rhyme!

Sarah Paulson

UNTITLED

Have you ever felt your heart beat
When you wake at night
The cool sweat upon your brow
Warming up with fright?
You sense a presence near you
Your hair begins to creep
You want to close your eyes again
Pretend to be asleep.

The thumping pulse within your chest
Is pounding in your head
Your body feels like iron
Bolted to the bed
The air is bursting in your lungs
You dare not let it slip
The fear is automatic
It has you in its grip.

Then your wide eyes focus
To search the darkened room
Everything is as it was
Showing through the gloom
As the fear is slowly lifted
You ease down on your side
And once again go back to sleep
With one eye open wide.

Peter H Kilby

KIDS OF TODAY

'Kids of today are bad,' some might say,
But I say 'What makes them that way?'
They have nothing to do once home from school,
So they hang around parks playing the fool!
What attitudes do you expect,
From adolescent children that feel neglect
From parents and the community alike?
It's high time adults made a positive strike,
Towards giving children something rewarding to do,
Instead of saying to them 'I know it was you!'

Michelle Hanstock

THE BOMB

What is blue mother?
Blue was the sky, child!
What is green mother?
Green was grass and trees child!
What are trees mother?
Trees were breath and life child!
Where are they now mother?
Gone child, gone for ever!
What is love mother?
Love is my lullaby for you child!
Hush now and sleep
Sleep on forever
Do not wake to this evil
This evil cloud of *death!*

C M Bellamy

THE MOTH

See how the moth fights against the flame,
My love for you, it's just the same.
Caught within your magnetic state,
Once again, it's love or hate.
How can you remain so unmoved,
When I decide it's me who's doomed,
What will happen? Will I always be . . .
An unwilling captive to your luminosity?

Susan Stokoe

GUARDIAN OF THE COE

Amongst the clouds they stand,
Skilfully crafted by nature's hand.
Through winter's snow and summer's sun,
as seasons come and seasons go.

People come to stand and stare,
but these sentinels of grey they do'nae care.
For thousands of years they have stood,
observing all that is bad or good.
Though history cuts deep it leaves no scar,
for these brooding giants so near yet so far.

The seasons and the years will pass,
effecting little this great grey mass.
Standing tall grey and proud,
whilst covered in a mist-like shroud.
The burn may run and the river race,
but for the guardian of them all this is the
final resting place.

Paul McNeil

IT'S TIME TO GO

Lying in my bed
Thinking of my friends and relatives
Of times past, both happy and sad
Moaning, groaning in agony
Crying tears, full of pain
Receiving tender loving care
From people who genuinely care
Feeding, changing, tucking-in
Receiving injections and pills regularly
Always heavily drugged
Days never-ending
Nights are never there
Visitors call in but never stay
Some a few minutes, a few a couple of hours
I wish they would go away
But I want them here and near

Sun shines, snow falls
Rain drizzles, wind howls
Green fields, perfumed flowers galore
Trees and shrubs
Dogs barking, cats meowing
Sheep bleating, cattle lowing
Birds in flight, singing their song
Sons and daughters
Spouses and children
I'll miss them all

I hear my name from afar
God is calling -
It's time to go!

Margaret Monaghan

A CHRISTMAS WISH

I look out of the window, the snow is falling down
So soft and lovely as it rests upon the ground
As I look at the moon the stars are shining bright
It is Christmas Eve at this special time of night
Father Christmas, down the chimney he comes
Leaving presents for everyone
Young and old people all excited the same
Because on Christmas morning
All the presents they will gain
Among the decorations upon the Christmas tree
There's a special little present lying there for me
I unwrap the shiny paper and see to my surprise
A little golden box with crystal shaped like eyes
As I open it music fills my ears
So beautiful and lovely nearly bringing me to tears
I see a little ballerina dancing round and round
Some swans are on a lake, so beautiful the sound
I look at all my cards, village scenes covered with snow
Cartoons and baubles tied up with a bow
I think of all the families having so much fun
Yet others in poor countries who are having none
I take a moment thinking of those people on their own
Those without a family or friends or those without a home
If we could all donate a gift to those who don't have one
We could have a chance to see the underprivileged having fun.

Sarah M Monaghan

THE BATTLE

Upon a hill, in pensive mood,
Of ancient times I start to brood.
I recall our knights of old
Brave and fearless - very bold.

Fighting here upon these hills,
Sword to shield and battling wills.
Fighting for their king and land,
Advancing bravely - sword in hand.

The noise of battle - metal clashing -
Horses neighing - strong arms thrashing -
Screams of pain and the bugle call -
Clouds of dust which cover all!
Crimson blood begins to flow -
The heat of battle seems to grow!
Armour glinting in the sun -
Fighting until the battle's won!

At last it's over - weary men
Return to camp - glorious again!
My thoughts return to the present day -
The sun has gone - the sky is grey.

I leave behind the battles of old.
The day - and battles - have now turned cold
As the ancient knights. I make my way
Homeward - the end of a glorious day.

S Taunton

VICTORY

A siren rang,
the noise was loud,
outside I watched,
a gathering crowd.
Down to the shelter!
I heard someone shout,
what was on my mind,
was how to get out.
Gas masks flying,
through the air,
pushing and shoving,
down the stairs.
Across to the shelter,
we ran for it,
I wasn't sure,
we all would fit.
I'd just got comfortable,
in my tiny space,
and just then,
there was another race.
Out onto the yard,
we all did go,
people running,
to and fro.
War was over,
we were free,
the siren rang again,
for *victory!*

Jennifer Paynter

WET SUMMER 1987

In twenty years' time they'll think of this day
And turn to each other and wistfully say,
'Remember that summer at Gorleston-on-Sea,
When we danced in the waves and the sun shone all day.'
Forgotten the days when it rained (how it poured).
'Til the sky joined the sea and the rain lashed the shore.
Forgotten the days when they peered through the panes,
Waiting with hope as it rains and it rains.
Now all they remember - one day of their stay,
When the beach rang with laughter -
And the sun shone all day.

Barbara E Dowdeswell

NORFOLK

Along the river bank I strode
Thro' reeds tall grass and bracken.
For company the sound of a croaking toad,
My pace I did not slacken.

The moist fresh air, damp atmosphere
Wet earth beneath my feet,
An easterly wind around my ears.
No soul was I to meet.

And yet at peace in this solitary place
No human to be heard or seen,
And far from being lonely,
Its purity strips the mind clean.

So many sounds in this lovely place,
Of creatures great and small,
Cows in the fields, birds in the trees
And the river running full.

Jean Bailey

A DAY AT THE SEASIDE

A world full of gloom.
A world full of doom.
Life is what you make it they say.
So come on and be happy for us today.

We are going for a day at the seaside.
Off we go in the car for a ride.
Yes here we are at the beach.
We come to a halt as the car brakes screech.

Off the kids go with their bucket and spade.
I think I'll just find a bit of shade.
I'll just get myself a deck chair.
I think it's alright to put it here.

Just about to sit down for a while
When up comes David with a sad smile.
Stephen's just kicked down my sand castle again.
Oh dear me! Isn't he a pain?

Never mind we'll have to build another one.
Just put this cream on if you're playing in the sun.
Come on let's build another sand castle for you,
Then we'll go in the water, will that do?

Wow! The water's cold as we put our feet in,
Splashing around the water is up to my chin.
Playing, running, forgetting about everything.
What happiness a day at the beach can bring.

Using all this energy I'm hungry and ready to eat.
Come on kids let's sit in the shade out of the heat.
Here we are some food and drink.
Fresh air has done you good your faces are pink.

On the way home they made not a peep.
As soon as their heads hit the pillow they were asleep.
Well what a wonderful day we all had.
Life can be so happy so don't feel so sad.

Kathy Buckley

CIRCE

Duty bids you sail away,
Drop all thought of leisure?
Can't you lose one single day,
Taste that much of pleasure?
Won't you for a little stay?
Stay for dinner, come what may.

Should devote your life to work,
So the killjoys say;
You should have the sense to shirk
If it hinders play;
They are fools who plough and dig,
Come, oh come, and be a pig.

Get your snout into the dish,
Gobble up the food,
It's exactly what I wish,
Tell you for your good:
Easy live and quiet die,
Come, oh come, into the sty.

Leave the horrid pain of thinking,
Let me set you free,
Life's for eating, sleeping, drinking,
Come and feast with me:
Six o'clock is when we dine,
Come and join the other swine.

Muriel Smith

THE EARTH'S AIR

Please be careful to my zone
Of air of plenty be
And don't let there be ignorance
Of the things that can hurt me

From CFCs and car exhausts
Dangers to me they are,
So please remember these few words
The next time you drive your car

CFCs from other things
Like sprays and fridges too;
Can put a hole into my layer
That later may hurt you

From heat to drought
I may spread wide;
Right around the globe;
Though this I would not wish

So help me please
To keep my shield
Which is all around your globe

I soon may mend
If an ear you'll lend,
From those who will advise;
So that none of these nasty things
Can reach up through the sky.

Ian B Wilkinson

FRIENDSHIP

A time of laughter
A time of tears
Those moments together
Will last for years

A time of sharing
A time to be fair
Friends will be there
In order to care

A time for disagreement
A time of space
Those moments
We've all faced

A time for silence
A time for thought
Endless memories
Of when we fought

A time for joy
A time for pain
Recollecting all
Down memory lane.

Nathalie El-Korashy

LOTTERY

Money, money, money
How would my life be
If my six numbers came up
On the weekend lottery?

Would it make me happy
Would it make me sad
Would it make me arrogant
Would it make me mad?

Would it make me brighter
Suave and full of charm
Would it do me lots of good
Or do me lots of harm?

I don't think I will risk it
I'll spend the pound on me
In the pub at happy hour
And stay in poverty.

L M Levey

SOUL MATES

I have two friends, and the love
they had it was never bad.
Our Lord above created their love.

Soul mates they are, and they've
come so far, to be together again.
But what a shame that they must part,
for he is taking some of her heart.
If only he could stay in this land,
but he has to take hold of God's hand.

So now they shall have to wait,
Until God makes them another date.

Margaret White

MY OPALINE MOON

A wandering sphere in the night sky
On which philosophers ponder and children do spy.
Dreaming lovers dance under its light
Whilst my *opaline moon* caresses the night.

The lost and the lonely look up to its face
Pin hopes to thoughts of its beauty and grace,
Chasing away our fears and our scars
As my *opaline moon* comforts the stars.

A crescent-shaped jewel that's just out of reach
Its siren like song pulls the waves to the beach,
And after the twilight's sweet lullaby is sung
My *opaline moon* serenades the dark sun

A terrestrial beauty which inspires from above
Our mortal terrain longing for love.
My *opaline moon's* affair with the night
Is over when sun shrouds us in glorious light.

D J Pantry

THE LAST ROSE

One so beautiful in perfect bloom,
Now fading so soon

You are still very precious,
Holding memories of summer inside your
dying petals

With the summer's passing you are gone,
Together with my heart which you have won.

A Giles

DREAM FLIGHT

I often dream
That I can fly
Amid the clouds
Way up high

I glide over rivers
And fields of green
Through luscious valleys
So rarely seen

An unspoilt paradise
As in days of old
What a wondrous sight
For one to behold

Like the Garden of Eden
Or so it would seem
Why can't it be real
Instead of a dream?

David Ross

UNTITLED

Lonely traveller
with the dusty feet
I raise my eyes to the sun
under the straw hat:
The sky is vast,
and unmoved.
So, I'll cross this other bridge,
I'll leave another county behind.
The horizon stretches in front of me
and I have all my life
to walk.

Elizabetta Bate

THE VISITOR

One morning very early
when I opened my front door,
I went to bring the milk in
and guess what I saw?
Laid upon the pavement
was a round prickly ball.
I said 'Good morning hedgehog,
how nice of you to call.'
He slowly unrolled before me
and opened his sleepy eyes
then he looked up at me
and gave a little sigh.
I stroked his little head
and said 'Would you like a drink?'
'Oh yes - some water please
as milk's too rich I think.'
I went and got some water
and a little chopped up meat
and gave it to the hedgehog
who said 'What a lovely treat!'
He ate it very slowly and said
'You're very kind,
friends like you are very hard to find!'
After he had finished
he said he must be on his way
'But I will come and see you another sunny day.'
He was such a cheery fellow
and I heard him give a laugh
as I stood by and watched him walk
down the garden path.

Sylvia Hardie

PRESTON MARKET

Heavy in build, she made her way
Through the market place that day
Legs swollen, bound up with cloth,
Bags in hand, she wasn't a toff.

Who was this dear, hobbling along
Making her way through the busy throng?
Had she been young in days that were gone,
Limbs that were swollen, been firm and strong?

Had she walked with a mother dear,
Run through lanes, full of cheer,
Had a young man, held her hand
Looked ahead as both had planned?

Who was the dear, struggling on
Making her way, through the busy throng?
Was she thinking now ahead,
To the time when she'd be dead
Or did memories of days gone by
Give light once more to the fading eye?

Someone's daughter, mother, wife,
Struggles on in the *game of life!*

H Kendle

SNOWFLAKES ARE HUMANS TOO

Celestial snowflake once released
gently floats; bringing silent peace

Millions, each unique; descending, ever dancing
Wind blowing flakes; posing, prancing

Landing softly, flakes form snow, the mass
To be moulded shaped, rejected; never last

Sunshine, snow evaporates; climbs to blue azure
Clouds gather, brings the celestial dance; once more.

Cars, omnibus and railway station
bring *unique individuals* to their destination

The autonomous beings arrive in the city
The millions now form the *sea of humanity.*

To be moulded, shaped, rejected; no charity

Five chimes, set free humanity, reverts; *liberty*
To prepare for next day and; . . . re-entry.

J W O Boyle

SNOW

Snow. Fleeting flowers, filigrees and fairy ferns;
each different from the other, tiny little falling
flakes, hexagon in style and shape covering the
world in a soft mantle of white, dropping silently
from feather'd clouds; darkened by bleak winter
skies, and it is as if the world has gone to sleep;
for you no longer hear the traffic's roar and here
and there we see a scarlet laden bush and snowdrops
standing in silent woods, but all too soon the winter
rain comes to wash it all away again, but not before
the children have played upon its marshmallow
crests and waves, their shouts of glee and joy
shattering the silence of long winter days before
Mother nature changes her dress and dons her cap of
multi-coloured loveliness, unlocking the frozen earth
until winter comes again spreading its gossamer white
upon everything in sight.

Agnes Mae

AUTO FRENZY

Environment friendly lead-free fuel,
The aim of the motor car is to rule
The lives of the people in every nation,
To celebrate a mechanical creation.
No public transport is plain to see,
Increases motor necessity.
This status symbol of the road,
Perpetuates the pollution load.
Extended motorways over fields,
Gives public demand that cause to yield.
With advertisements promising dreams,
Listen, can you hear the screams
Of a world with engines choking?
Ban the car, you must be joking!

David K Green

MEMORIES

Memories are within us all
Good memories and the bad
The good ones make us happy
The bad ones often sad
We cannot keep the good ones
And dismiss the sad ones, no
For they are built within us
And it ever will be so
For it is in daily situations
That the memory seeds are sown
And each one has its garden
In which the seeds will grow.

A W Bartram

IF

If only I had waited
If only you had called
If only are the words that say it all.

If only I had thought
If only you could see
If only means we grew apart
If only down to me.

If only we could meet
If only to talk it out
If only we could be friends
If only to sort it out.

If only I didn't love you
If only for a while
If only means we grew apart
If only is a broken heart.

If only means I'm sorry
If only you could see
I didn't mean to destroy us
If only - *yes, it's me . . .*

Christine Mountney

FOXGLOVES

Towering purple spikes,
Elevated elegance on forest bank
Against a haven of green and brown,
Vying for light.
Proud sunlit grace,
Purple fantasia.

Marion L D Rooke

MAN

The countryside belongs to you and me,
From the tiniest insect, to the smallest tree,
Bluebells, primroses, the wild flowers we seek,
Mother nature's overwhelming beauty we peep.

The landscape's changing, the land is being sold,
We must make room for progress, or so we are told,
But what cost to nature, man's everlasting greed,
The trees, the flowers, the animals . . .
Don't they also have a need?

Denise Tong

LIFE

Things can go wrong, as they so often do,
Why? No-one has ever found the clue,
Money's tight, and the debts start to rise,
We sit dumbfounded, stare and cry.

Life is strange and just as unpredictable to one and all,
And, it seems that sometimes we just need that fall,
To find out exactly what's more precious to us,
Money, happiness, family, or basic trust.

The trust we need to be able to strive on,
The trust in our family, friends, and God,
Together: nothing seems so hard, or all that bad,
So dust yourself down, smile at life and be glad.

We're alive, and here to stay,
Often things change day by day,
Life is precious, of that there's not a doubt,
Carry on, we all sometimes have to get turned inside out.

Albert A Thompson

THE LITTLE BEE

Yesterday when I was having my tea
a flipping bee kept pestering me.
I tried to be gentle, showing it the door
then the little darling stung me
so I swatted it to the floor.
As I watched it wriggling around
hither and thither upon the ground
I thought, the poor little thing is dying
and from its sting I was still crying
but I couldn't bear to watch it die
so wiping a tear from my eye
I swept it up on a bit of paper
put it outside, but when I checked later
the little bee had passed away
it did not live to see another day.
I started to feel really sorry
for what I had done
Oh, I know killing a little bee
wouldn't bother some.
Then as its sting started to fester on my leg
I was flipping glad that bee was dead.

Heather Hepburn

THE ORCHARD

Down by the orchard on a Saturday morning
In my tent when the day is dawning
There are ducks down by the stream
It's so quiet, am I in a dream?
It's good to be in the country day or night
Hedgehogs, badgers and bats don't give me a fright.
I love to be in the country I don't want to go
It's nice to be in the country, *that I know!*

Christopher Johnson (8)

LOVE IS . . .

Like a bird caged inside your body,
Flapping wings to set it free.
Like tight elastic round your chest.
Like rippling waves across the sea.
Love is . . .

Like an unknown burst of light
Captured in your brain.
Like a surge of power,
Decreasing gloom and pain.
Love is . . .

Encased inside a web of wonder.
A fantasy, it seems.
The only reassurance
Of what life really means
Love is . . .

The touch that makes you shudder,.
Kissed lips that turn to ice.
The warmth of bodies one to one.
It's more than nice,
Love is . . .

A broken heart, a tearful night,
The pain can't be explained.
A sad farewell, a final kiss
With which all hopes are drained.
For we have lost the magic key
That locks our hearts together.
So as we say goodbye, we know
We say goodbye for ever.
Love is the one thing that I miss
Love is . . .

Heather Cheney

FRIENDS

When the chips are down, when you're really low
That is when you know your friends, they will show
Who they are they don't judge you . . . they stay,
And don't begrudge you chances that come your way.
They are just true friends come what may . . .they stay.

They are there for you, are worthy and true
Fair-weather friends are there when times are good
But true pals are there when all others forsake you.
I have a Friend, He is there for me, I look at Him come
what may
And I know that *He* will stay.

Linda Guest

REDEVELOPMENT

What peace I feel when I look round these fields,
Each acre is different, with the beauty it yields.
The cows look so happy as they chew their way round,
The birds fill the air with their magical sound.
Why must we build houses and roads on each space?
Is our intention to destroy the human race?
For with each tree felled and every field that is dug,
On the ozone layer sadly, we're pulling the plug.
I could understand all this building if there was a need,
But half will lie empty, so it's just down to greed.
When will we wake up and enjoy what we've got?
Not self-destruct, but be content with our lot.
Our great grandchildren's future, lies in our hands,
So we must stop now! Destroying these lands.

Jennyen

ANGUISH . . .

The empty line
Hides my divine.
So not tonight
To hold her tight.
The tears build up behind my eyes,
The call of curlew, hides my cries.
In anguish, I just beat the stone
As I stand in darkness, all alone.
I cast my curses on the fell.
Oh, pray the sheep could go and tell,
That I alone am stood out here.
For just one second, please, my dear
Come out, and let me feel your breath
Blow across the field and hold its warmth.
Through those thick walls the bond is true.
Barbed wire nor bog keep me from you.
Relax. To sleep I'll go, beneath the stars
Relax. No fuss. Tomorrow is, the day for us.

Robert J Hodgson

EXTRA BITS

I'd like to design my own body
And fit it with some zips
Then I wouldn't need a doctor
To sort out all my bits.

It would be so much easier
If I could take them out myself
I'd put them in a pickle jar
And leave them on the shelf.

If ever I needed them again
I could put them all back in
Or if they're past their sell-by date
I would put them in the bin.

I'd also drill my joints with holes
And add a couple of hinges
Then get a can and oil myself
Whenever I get the twinges.

S Wheeler

ANGEL IN THE NIGHT

She's an angel in the night,
When she leaves her palace walls.
She's an angel in the night,
When she hears their distressed calls.

For she's called the Queen of Hearts
And she listens to their pleas.
For she's called the Queen of Hearts
(With children at her knees)

With no love to call her own
She must face the silent night.
So with no love to call her own
She must ease another's plight.

For she's called the Queen of Hearts
and she's an angel in the night.

James G Goodwin

REASONS

Life doesn't seem worth living now that you are gone.
It's hard to pick up the pieces and find strength to carry on,
Days are now just meaningless night-time so forlorn,
I ask is there a reason for me to carry on.
Then a little hand slips gently into mine
A loving face looks up and asks 'Mummy
Why are you crying?'
I hug this little boy who looks so much like you
He's the reason why, I have to see life through.

Frances Murray

COLOURS OF MY HEART

The sea is green,
The sky is blue,
I'll mix my emotions with a colour for you,
Maybe dark green,
Maybe brown,
All these colours would make you frown,
I'll take the whole of my heart,
And then begin right from the start,
I'll shade it in a very light pink,
To make you stop and even think,
There are no colours for me or you,
It's just another way of saying 'I love you.'

Diana L Woodcock

THE SEASONS CHANGE

The sun rising slowly in the sky
Tells us that a new day is nigh.
Fair day dawns clear and bright,
The countryside a glorious sight.
A vibrant orange, a burnished gold
Such wondrous colours to behold.
Autumn is here, the time is right
For trees to change colour overnight.

The morning dew sparkles on the grass,
The pond water reflects the sun like glass.
The cobwebs hanging in the trees,
Avoided by the industrious bees,
Look like necklaces of silver and agate
As dew and sunlight integrate.
The scent of flowers wafts on the breeze
As squirrels scamper through the leafy trees.

In a few short weeks the scene will alter,
As winter comes the weather will falter.
Sun will change to cloud, rain or frost,
And most colourful flowers will be lost.
We must now face the winter's storms
'Til once again the weather warms
When once again a spring dawn will bring
Bluebells and birds singing on the wing.

Edward Hall

MISTY AUTUMN LAND

Misty autumn land all aglow
Thoughts of winter snow
Crackling logs bonfire smoke
Mist and rain to soak
All the autumn season delights
Harvest gather, bird in flight
Homewards to warmer lands
Darkening night to be found
Misty daylight breaks slumber
Long not awake.
Nature turning through time
Ready for cold bleak days
Time for hoarding ways
Pots of jammy delight
Put away for winter tea by
Fire glow harvest hoard
Stored away hats and gloves
To keep us warm today all
This season will come and go
And still the soft white
Winter snow.

L Wayth

AFTER THE WAR?

His steel face glitters as he glares from rubble
A soldier disfigured by fire,
A toy deserter, a casualty of war,
Homeless, his grave is the charcoals of life.

Mountains of dust mark the maps of streets,
As families inspect the loss.
A photograph kisses a pool in the street,
Half burnt, half torn, lost, they lie.

Red, white and blue replaces black, grey and brown
Cries, and screams of sadness turn to joy.
The world creeps from corners and sighs
And the toy soldier's face draws a crooked smile.

Dawn Prescott

FRIENDSHIP

Friendship is a thing, that money cannot buy,
You really have to earn it, so somehow you must try,
To make yourself acceptable, and this will make you proud,
Without some you'll feel miserable, feel lonely in a crowd.

Friendship is a lovely word, it's music to one's ear,
Money cannot buy it, yet it fills you full of cheer,
For be ye black or be ye white, be little or be tall,
You've really got to have a friend, without them you may fall.

Friendship's all around you, if you really try to be
A kind and gentle person, who wants to help to free,
Those poor and so unfortunate souls, who wallow in distress,
Who cannot seem to find their feet, when in a sordid mess.

Friendship can't be beaten, when you're at your lowest ebb,
Things seem bad, you can't go on, you're caught up in a web,
So some kind deed, or from the heart, a gently spoken word,
Could make someone feel wonderful, in their dark and dismal world.

Friendship feels so wonderful, when you hold your arms wide,
Embrace someone less fortunate, who's on the downward slide,
Show to them a brighter life, and once more they'll feel grand,
When you give out lots of friendship, and lend a helping hand.

Sandy Laird

LORDS OF THE SEA

Oh! Gentle *lords* of the restless sea
enchanted are my heart and soul by thee
as I hear thy sweet song of liberty

It carries me across the oceans far and wide
through waters blue and green upon the tide
to where thou doth wander and reside
gentle *lords* of the sea.

Oh! Gentle *lords* of the earth's ocean
my heart sings with a heavenly emotion
as though enraptured by a magic potion.

A voyager 'neath the seas of imagination
steered by a dreaming captain's navigation
toward a union of minds in communication
with thee, gentle *lords* of the sea.

Oh! Gentle *lords* of the restless deep
with thee I roam in the realms of sleep
thy haunting song makes my heart weep.

For storm clouds are gathering in the sky
a warning that your race is doomed to die
by the hand of *man* who will not cry
when thou are gone, *lords* of the sea.

Oh! Gentle *lords* of the restless sea
I pray our lost companions thou will not be.
Shall I never hear again thy song of liberty?

For to lose thy beauty would break my heart
if from the great oceans thou did depart
the seas would be empty, cold and dark
without thee, gentle *lords* of the sea.

Paul Crudginton

SNOW

Snow falls slowly to the ground
Not a footstep to be found
The ground outside covered white
So pure and clean and beautifully bright.

Children run outside to play
Isn't it a lovely snowy white day?
Snowmen built all around
Now there's little snow on the ground.

Small footsteps trodden everywhere
Disturbed the wintry snowy white glare
No more clear white sheet of snow
Just a slushy mess that will finally go.

Until it starts to melt away
The snowmen stay for another day
A while it takes to melt it down
First it starts to lose its crown

The stones for eyes have now fell
What it is now it's hard to tell
The carrot nose is on the ground
In the melted snow that lies around.

Buttons fall one by one
Until, finally the snowman's gone
What a shame he had to go
All that's left is the melted snow.

E Hatfield

MADDEN HALL

By distant hills lies Gallop Moor.
I recommend that you explore.
Upon the heights, behind the wall,
the baron's stronghold Madden Hall.
So well preserved as you will find
with artefacts of every kind.

The tourists pay and take a peek
while children play at hide and seek.
In every room the guardians stand
to answer questions they're on hand
in costumes dressed to match the age
some ladies, henchmen and a page.

The kitchen now quite silent stands
where food was cooked by many hands
much wine and victuals for the feast
some sixteen courses at the least.
A fireplace, though devoid of coal
where once an ox was roasted whole.

The guardian here is rather pale
as though he's just come out of jail.
No 'by your leave' or 'do you mind?'
My children pose, he stands behind.
When snaps return we only stare
our new-found friend's no longer there.

Brian Kelly

MY LOVING FRIEND

You give me all your love and trust,
And I don't know why you feel you must,
You're always there when I feel down,
You always smile and never frown,
You're always there when I feel low,
It always seems as if you know,
That life can be so cruel sometimes,
And that it helps to write these rhymes,
You're always there my loving friend,
But all good things one day must end,
For everyone some day must die,
And I know that I should not cry,
For you'll still live on in my heart,
But, 'Oh,' the sadness when we part,
Your soul, I know, still carries on,
So I won't mourn when you are gone,
I know we'll meet again some day,
Some other place along the way,
And when we do, we'll both be glad,
And reminisce of times we had,
But until then I know you're there,
To come to me and show you care,
To bring me joy and try to please,
To bring my life a little ease,
Because I know your kind of love,
Comes from the heart, not from above.

Bruce Simpson

ONE DREAM

The tick of the clock, I hear it so clear,
Every second, every hour, then, another heartache appears.
Farewell to my dream, my silent desire,
Gone is the sparkle that lit my fire.
What is this craving that I behold, the longing of our
Child to love.
To dress, to feed, to care, to hold, with the most
undenying love.
To be a zombie would simply be fine,
There would be no clock to tick in my mind.
No feelings of bitterness, pain or despair,
In my childless existence as I climb life's stairs.
No havoc or heartache would our child bring,
But a sense of commitment and a sign of good things.
Within my partner I could not ask for more,
I have all I need, then - a little more.
Our love for each other is wholesome and true,
I whisper the words to him, 'I love you.'
But in the quiet of the day and the silence of night,
I am alone with my heartache as it reaches great heights.
Should my dream thus appear, would my partner remain,
To share the enjoyment of a family domain.
So deep is my love, yet I could never remove,
A life if bestowed within the depths of my womb.
Would he stay with me and release his fear, if our love became one,
And our child appeared.

Gill

THE DARK SIDE OF NIGHT

An albatross soars above the waves,
Ghostly galleons stir in their watery graves,
The moonlight weaves in and out of the sea,
And on this night the spirits are set free.

They wander and roam through the ghostly town,
They leave a trail of frost on the cobbled ground,
And as the clock strikes twelve,
The hour of the brave,
The souls stir gently in their graves.

Then as the sky gets light,
And dawn draws near,
The apparitions disappear.

Samantha Betts (14)

UNTITLED

Wandering the streets
Full of lost thoughts and dreams
Lonesome, not a person
How simple this life seems

Fears and hopes
United as one
In the land of darkness
Awaiting the sun that has gone

Eternal footsteps
Time pushes on
Daylight breaks
Then all is re-begun

Stefanie Moore

REFLECTIONS

As the years slip away like a swift running stream
And the winters seem churlish and cold.
And there's no urgent wish to be up and away
Then I realise - I'm getting old.

Yet within me a spirit burns - steadfast and bright -
Never heeding the hurrying years.
Still eager to share in each passing delight
And rebuking old age for its fears.

I can laugh with a child, and feel youthful as he -
I can weep at his childish despair
I can sigh with a lover who loses his love
And feel all the pain he must bear.

I can thrill to the joy of a morning in spring
And exult at the song of the birds.
And a passage of music can move me to tears
Or a poet's evocative words.

It's the word left unspoken - the journey not made
One regrets when the moment has gone
And the realisation that time is too short
To encompass what one might have done

But the loves I have had, and the joys I have known
Will enrich all my days to the end.
And when death comes at last to wind up life's brief day
May I greet him - with trust - as a friend.

Ivy Collins

A MORNING WALK

I wander down a once quiet road
Traffic now roaring by
I pass the houses, quiet and still
under the early morning sky

The trees and hedges sparkling with dew
The flowers not yet awake
But always the traffic roaring by
who has this journey to take?

The rest of the town is still sleeping
The birds just starting to sing
The journeys continue, in lorry and car
taking their drivers near and far
I turn and retrace my steps with a sigh
A once peaceful morning walk is no more
Now that the traffic can go roaring by.

M Laverty

TO SMELL THE SUMMER

Inside the days, inside the week
I tasted flowers

Flowers like I'd never seen a dream of colours
rich, deep full

Pulling petals we pressed into the clay
always I'll remember

September the week we dressed a picture
only the stars can tell

To smell, to drink I breathed today
to smell the summer

Dan Donovan

A FOREST'S SOUL

Why are you weeping my forest?
Why so quiet and forlorn?
You're usually very busy
Watching new life be reborn!

Ancient oak, my old friend
Your leaves are shedding tears!
I've known you from a sapling
And that's been many years!

I've wrapped my arms around you
Oh so many times
You told me many secrets
That bought me peace of mind

But today you're cold and distant
And your voice I cannot hear!
You've always been my special friend
And our friendship's been so dear

I walked home feeling lonely
Perhaps I was to blame
Then, I cheerfully thought tomorrow
That past joys would be the same

But when it came the morning
I'd been so completely wrong
My forest had been massacred
And all my friends were gone

I would really like to tell you
What my friend revealed to me
But I feel it would be detrimental
To so-called humanity.

Elizabeth M Cook

THE HEADLESS HORSEMAN

He rode so valiant on his steed,
Shield and dagger at his every need,
The road where he walked when he had his head,
Now a pool of blood filled with sorrow and dread.

He died in his dark, tan breeches and ruff,
Found in an alley, a sleek, black glove,
His silver stallion, an illusion in the light,
His ruby red eyes that sparkle in the night.

A tragic death by a runaway tram,
A warm-hearted, kind and generous man,
A friend and protector, he never would lie,
It's more than a shame that a good man should die.

Now a whisper in the shadows?
Or an empty silhouette?
A flicker of ghostly silver,
Has he truly gone yet?

Kim Maddocks

TIME

Time steals the baby from the cradle,
Snatches the infant from its mother's arms,
Robs the young man of all his dreams
And plunders the maiden of her charms.

Time is the wife who becomes a widow,
The father who was once known as a son,
A woman peering in the mirror,
The beginning and end of everyone.

J K Horne

CHRISTMAS MAGIC

'Twas the night before Christmas, calm, crisp and bright.
Jack Frost had dappled the trees all in white.
The hearth where I sat gave a warm cosy glow,
which shone on the stockings that hung in a row.

The children were sleeping and close by each head,
their Teddy was lying tucked up in the bed.
As the clock struck on midnight - not one second before,
Our kitten Oliver came through the door.

'Hiel-ll-iow' he greeted, as plain as can be,
and I stared in amazement as he looked at me.
An old lady once told me that on each Christmas Eve,
the animals spoke (which I didn't believe).

'Hello Olli,' I answered as he crossed the floor,
'Go iouwt?' he asked, as he neared the front door.
About an hour later when I let him back in,
'How was your evening?' I enquired, with a grin.

'Mieow' he replied, 'twas the best he could do!
But I know what I heard, and I swear that it's true.
Outside I saw Santa sat in his sleigh,
and he gave a broad wink just as he drove away.

Now I know what you're thinking! With the Sherry and all,
the story I'm telling must sound very tall!
But I know what I heard, and I swear that it's true,
and I hope that one Christmas it will happen to you.

William Latham

FIRST SNOWFLAKE

Dull grey clouds filled the wintry
sky,
The silent birds went quickly flying
by.
The last autumn flower head bent
down,
Trembled, as the snowflake fell upon
the ground.
Softly they fell, till everything
turned white,
The earth had found its lover, that
still and starless night.
Held in the arms of nature, caressed
by the falling snow,
She conceived in that night of silence,
the seeds that in spring would grow.

Maurice Kean-Cockburn (Deceased)

THINGS I LIKE

I like the day to come.
I like the birds that sing.
I like the bees that hum.
I like the trees and flowers too.
I like to hop I like to skip.
I like to play all day through.
I like to dance I like to sing.
I like to go to school.
I like the night when it gets dark.
I like the stars that shine so bright.
I like the moon lighting up the sky.
I like my comfy bed at night,
Especially in the wintertime.

Laura-Jayne Cregg (10)

TWIN TOWERS

As the sun rises over the mighty cathedral
a groundsman strolls over the hallowed ground
nurturing, tending his love never-ending
for this sacred place to a passionate crowd

The anthems and hymns echo from the past
in roaring dedication to those with pride
who played their hearts out for their team and country
and held their heads high for the ultimate prize

The twin towers soar with flags flying high
reaching up towards the heavens above
like guardian angels protecting their most
important of places which so many love

Some say it's just a concrete stadium
but the heart of every Englishman says
'No it's more than any words can convey
there is only one place where dreams are made'
. . . Wembley

Sandra Petch

RAT RACE

Confined to a wheelchair all of the day,
How I wish I could get up and walk away.
A lot of the pain I've learned to bear,
but what hurts most, is when people stare.
Going along pushing my wheels, trying to ignore
the sound of heels.
To get to the front they all push past,
no prize for guessing who's going to be last.

Jagraj Poseley

ARKLE THE RACEHORSE

Have you heard of a horse called Arkle?
To the racetrack he added sparkle,
full of blinding speed
and rippling muscle
against other horses he had to tussle.

Jumping fences like a deer
He's won again four lengths clear
entering the winner's enclosure
He held his head up high
as if saying with a snort
those others could not get by

The jockey laughed and remarked
he went a fast pace
in the end it was a one-horse-race
a proud owner gave him a kiss
saying what a fine boy you are
then his trainer gave him a pat
knowing he would go far.

Y P Bacon

ALONE

I am alone within myself
like a tree within the woods.
I am like a nightingale's song
trapped within a pigeon's breast.
The tears run down my cheeks
like the rain falls in the night.
Life itself extinguishes my will to live
so I sit here waiting to die.

TAJ

MY GARDEN

If I had a little garden
Oh! How happy I would be
To sit among the trees and flowers
Would be just the thing for me
To hear the birds a-singing
In the trees way up above,
Would be like heaven to me,
And my garden, I would love.
One day maybe my wish
May come true.
If you wish hard enough,
Sometimes they do.

Jean Brown

THE WEEPING WILLOW

Oh weeping willow why so sad?
Surely life cannot be so bad?
Look up look all around, take your head up from the ground
The wind is rushing and scuttling through the leaves
Look up and watch the buzzing bees
Get up and come alive, watch the bees working in their hive
Weeping willow with head hung low,
Sweeping coloured leaves o-so-slow
He's sometimes by the riverbank and sometimes in the park
But always when I see the weeping willow
He is singing like a lark.

Kathryn Earls

REFLECTIONS

'Twas just six weeks ago today
A perfect stranger came my way
He asked if he could dance with me
I did, he said 'reluctantly.'
He was a dark and handsome man
And then a brief romance began.

But as we moved around the floor
We danced more closely than before
We joked and laughed, he sang a lot
Saying in his boot my car he'd pop.
We danced all night, the hour was late
Was it chance, I thought 'twas fate!

He saw me home and said he'd ring
And chemistry's another thing
It seemed so right just being there
A sort of magic in the air
Attracted to each other by sight
Two lonely strangers in the night.

He duly rang, we made a tryst
Both arrived early, was I at risk?
We to his dwelling place did go
Feeling vulnerable, I don't know
I sipped some wine and settled down
And snuggled up his arm around.

I hear a flippancy of tongue
A capricious manner, I feel is wrong
A method of self-defence, he says
But surely there are other ways
I've made a try at understanding
But I find it too demanding.

Joyce B Livingstone

DRIVEN TO DESPAIR

This is the wheel, here are the pedals
Now, just turn on the ignition
Push down gently, there, you're away
This is the beginning of your tuition.

Oh my God, what am I doing
I'm on the move, and so's the perspiration
My hands are glued around the wheel
Already the instructor's into frustration.

A figure of eight, around we go
Only fifty-five minutes to the end
Of this charade, I must be mad
This lesson is driving me round the bend.

Am I doing this right? My teeth are clenching
Will this nightmare ever go away
Or am I doomed to go round and round
While I grasp the wheel and pray.

There you are, now we'll go home
You've made a very good start
See you next week, for your next lesson
Oh, be still my beating heart . . .

Wynne McLaren

THE CIRCLE OF LIGHT

Oh what a pretty sight
Is the circle of light
Though it shines so bright
Through the darkest of nights.

But it gives you a fright,
Because it twinkles so nice,
So it comes to me,
In the middle of the night.

If only I knew,
What it wanted from me.
But it could be the key,
To succeed in dreams.

So when I awake,
I would know what it meant.
Or is it message,
Heaven sent.

M Vale

LOOKING OUT IN THE DARK NIGHT

Looking out in the dark night I hear not a sound,
The houses with no lights on stand all around,

The street light glaring their bright yellow beams
This night is not as quiet as it seems.

I look to the moon and the stars up above,
this night just seems the right one for love.

Not a cloud in the sky, just a slight breeze in the air,
Just wish any wish and it will be there.

A couple stroll past, hand in hand,
I think to myself isn't love grand.

As I shut my window and close the curtains tight
I get into my bed and say my prayers for the night.

B M Cook

WIND'S JOURNEY

Escaping breezes softly blowing
Breathing clouds in a faint blue sky,
Fleeting the ground, blowing foliage
Murmuring tones of essence, ever near.
Swiftly changing warmer, colder
Formulating pageants before our eyes
Skyline colours, delicately falling
Far in the distance, nature's voice.
Hungrily dashing the untrodden pathways
Blowing trees with unspoilt clamour
Whipping, quivering, changing weather
Returning to calmness and resting sound.

W Goddard

UNTITLED

Love could make poets of us all,
if only we would let it.
But if we did, what would befall
all those who are indebted,
for inspiration to love's call,
so they can write, to please us all,
of passions pure and otherwise,
soft words, flowers, clear blue skies?

Would they then resort to writing about
sensible things
in order to keep their bank balances
in the black?

B Cox

TIME

Time waits for no-one, you know it's true
but hours that pass have their own time too
For some, the day may seem forever
for lovers, it's not long enough together.
And when a loved one is far away
every hour seems like a day.
Time is relative to what you do
and the friends you have are important too.
If you're lucky and love your work
the time goes quickly without a quirk
but if you hate every working hour
time drags on and makes you sour.
Night-time too can be unforgiving
for those whose sleep is overridden,
as many thoughts revive in the pitch black
of memories and regrets from sometime back.
The hours in the night or the day
depend on contentment in a way.
Finally, it means nothing as we wend
towards the peace of journey's end.

Roger Hoar

JAMES

A little soul, like no other,
So much joy, from one little boy.
He shall never see a brother,
nor play with even one little toy.
He was the first, a special young man,
Pictures were taken, especially of you.
Sweet little baby belonging to Ann,
Think of you often, we always will do.

Jean Hamer

THE GLASS

Bright and shiny
glowing with pride
Perched on a sideboard
nothing to hide.

One minute it's there
the next it is gone
Accidents happen
and life must go on.

The glass is shattered
tiny fragments fly
so gentle are the
way they lie.

Swift to fall and
easy to break
The moment passes
through someone's mistake.

Sheree Goodman

MY TREASURE

My little girl can drive me wild,
She can be such a naughty child.
Around the shops it is hard to cope,
As she runs around, there is no hope.

She is gran and grandad's pride and joy,
They give her sweets and sometimes toys.
To them she is perfect in every way,
But they don't have her 24 hours a day.

They come and play with her for an hour,
To them she is a most precious flower.
Then when they leave and we are on our own,
She starts again to wreck our home.

And now it is time for her to go to bed,
She is washed and clean, she has been fed.
After running me right off my feet,
My daughter is so lovely, now she's asleep.

Doreen Lough

UNTITLED

It's five o'clock on Christmas morn
The time that parents dread
When all the children wake up
And jump upon your bed

No more rest will you get today
Because Santa Claus has been
There's parcels to unwrap
And presents to be seen

But you join in the spirit
And enjoy their fun
Because you can remember
The days when you were young

You see their smiling faces
As they play upon the floor
You hear their happy laughter
How could you ask for more

And all those days you've worried
How you could make their day
Has paid off with abundance
Their happiness your pay

And with shining eyes they thank you
Then in your heart you're glad
You've got those lovely children
And you are their mum and dad

B S Todd

LIFE

Hidden from the sight of man,
The reasons for our being.
Although we search the universe,
It's not within our seeing.
The searching starts
From man's first breath,
For secrets better hid.
It carries on to final death,
When all is then revealed,
And all the hopes, and all the dreams
That stretch back over time,
And all the worldly plans and schemes,
Are placed before our sight.

Robert Selby

VANDAL

I walked in the same shoes as you,
All across the songs you like -
Left footprints in the lyrics,
Kicked chords out of key.

I walked in the same places as you,
In the courts and gardens -
Left footprints in the stones,
Carved symbols on the trees.

I walked round your head in your shoes,
Cut a path through your mind -
Left footprints deep in memory
Trespassed on your life.

Susanna Forrest

MOVING ON

Dance with me, my lover,
To the music in my mind.
Dance with me forever,
Our bodies both entwined.

Run with me my lover,
Through valley and past tree.
Run with me, forever,
Release me, let me free.

Sleep with me my lover,
'tween sheets of satin, black.
Sleep with me forever,
There will be no turning back.

Mary Dowdeswell

THE JOKER'S FUNFAIR FANFARE

Wow! What a happy surprise!
Come here quickly,
You won't believe your eyes
The magical merry-making
Joker's funfair fanfare is here!
To entertain us all
At the Butterfly Ball!
Hooray! Hooray!
See the old men jump and shout
Whilst the dogs bark and run about.
The children laugh and shout for joy!
There'll be lots of fun and games
For every girl and boy
So come quickly! Run, run, run.
The Joker's mad, magical show has just begun!

Jason Davies

MOVIE SCREEN

One hundred years of the movie screen
We celebrate this year
One hundred years of magic seen
With many, many a tear

So many stars have made their mark
Within that world of make believe
From silent films, oh so stark
That made us laugh and made us grieve.

Slapstick comedy in all its fun
Took our minds from troubled days
Tales of love affairs begun
Left our hearts in a happy haze.

Where would we be without it now
To while away some pleasant hours
We owe so much to those who wow
and thrill us with their acting powers.

Jill Wiseman

SHEEP VANDALS

I wandered lonely as a sheep
That roams on high over vale and hills
Then all of us formed a crowd
And ate up all your daffodils.
You can spend lots of dosh, securing your gate
But to ruin your garden we cannot wait
Tens of us you will see at a glance.
We'll make you scream, shout and dance.
By your fence beneath your bush
If you've got flowers we'll push and push
But we'll find a way in just wait and see
Then munch upon your garden with glee!

Joanne Griffiths (11)

WHEN ALL IS SAID AND DONE

When all is said and done, the music still playing,
People around you everywhere, drowns out what
they are saying,
The music makes the moment, the music makes
you feel,
The music makes things special, then you don't want
what's real,
Turn off the music and everything seems so cold,
Heartless words that stab you like knives, and scar you
as you get old,
It hurts when others knock the emotions that you are
forever displaying,
Remember . . . when all is said and done
the music is still playing.

Holly Bradshaw

THE OAK TREE

Oh lusty lofty sturdy oak
    You strong and mighty tree,
To live the rings within your trunk
    And be as wise as thee.
You've weathered winds
    You've wintered hard,
You've seen much rise and fall,
    Your crusty bark is lightening scarred,
Yet still you're proud and tall.
    I hold you close with arms outstretched
And my heart beats close to thee.
    King of the forest oh mighty oak,
Much joy you hold for me.

J H Robins

UNSPOKEN 'TIL THE END

There is something very special
That must not stay unsaid.
I meant to tell you yesterday
But our sons came first instead.
I should have told you last week,
And the week before.
But with our 'little distractions'
The words were gone once more.
We have built our life together
And our family along the way,
Let's not neglect each other
So I'll take the time to say
Our few quiet moments together,
So very precious to the end.
I give you fully, all my love,
My husband and my friend.

Mary R T Hill

L*!#

Love is a four letter word
And is usually the least heard
Terms of endearment are whispered in your ear
To be overheard is the greatest fear

Love is a four letter word
And most men find it absurd
Ask him do you love me
Of course I love you is the key

Love is a four letter word
And if too mixed up it will curd
So be true and honest to your lover
Because you may not find another!

Susan Philbey

KEW

There was me.
I was alone in Kew Gardens.
A leaf fluttered gently by my ear and she appeared.
I spoke and said what nice weather it was.
It was not.
She said that it would improve.
It did and I commended her foresight.
She blushed.
I coughed.
She said did I come there often.
I said yes and did she not think it was a little bit of paradise.
She nodded and stood up to look at a blossoming Laburnum.
I stood up.
I moved next to her.
She took one step nearer to me to look closer at a group of petals.
I leant down also, but to put my cheek next to hers.
We looked into each other's eyes until I could feel her breath on the
bridge of my cold nose.
We kissed long and eagerly.
There was us.

Jonathan Wallace

POETRY IN MOTION

Poetry in motion
a word locomotion,
sublime transformations
of ordinary associations.

Poetry in motion
a rare combination
of word presentation
for your appreciation.

Emma Leigh

YOU NEVER TRIED

If you should ever wonder
What it's like to be afraid,
Or watch the self destruction
Of foundations that you've laid'
If you ever want to know
How it feels to be deceived
To watch the sudden downfall
Of success that you've achieved;

Just take a look at me and what happened when you lied.
Feel how I felt when all the hope had died.
See just what it was that made me run and hide.
You never even tried.

If you should ever wonder
Just how I made it through,
Wonder where I got the strength
To walk away from you,
If you ever want to know
What it was that made me cry,
What it was that made me hurt so much
That I had to say goodbye;

Just take a look at me and what happened when you lied.
Feel how I felt when all the hope had died.
See just what it was that made me run and hide.
You never even tried.

Alex Hutchinson

SO NEAR AND YET SO FAR

Life goes on yes I know it's true
But life's not the same Dad since we lost you
The sun still shines and the birds still sing
The flowers still grow in the early spring
As each day still dawns in the freshest dew
We will see your face it's the same old you
Why I asked myself did you suffer so
Yet you still fought on never letting go
Of your love for us in your special way
Waiting for the time when you slipped away
Leaving us for now to remember you
In our earthly home not the same without you
Yet you're near to us in your special way
At the start and end of our troubled day
The night will come as we whisper low
We love you Dad and we miss you so.

Pat Bolton

1914 -
FROM THE WESTERN FRONT

Do not mourn for me,
Do not cry,
For all that live,
Must also die.

Time is a healer,
Soon twill pass,
But never forget me,
My sweet bonny lass.

Tabitha Morgan

INSPIRED

Looking at the golden Sun;
Seeing it shine upon your hair,
I feel that I could go and run
Up with the birds, up in the air.

Look at it shine down on the Sea.
I turn, and see you smile.
I think about you and me,
But we can only stay a while.

Can you feel the magic here;
Or see the beauty of the rays?
I'd like to stay forever here,
I want to stay for days.

To be with you in winter heat,
To remain here in the glow . . .
I'm glad the Heavens helped us meet,
Now I never want to go.

Kerryn Ulyatt

THE WONDERS OF THE GARDEN

It is the morning; open your eyes and get out of bed.
Look out of your window to the day ahead.
For those who have been blessed with the gift of sight,
Unfolds before them a veritable delight.

How beautiful the rose is, the violet and lily too.
The wonders of the garden are there for you to view.
The robin with his red breast, for him there is no rest.
The nightingale up in the tree, singing her very best.

The grass so green, the air so clean; how peaceful life is here.
Sitting beneath the bowers, among so many flowers.
The colours of the rainbow at the break of dawn;

The morning dew glistening upon the lawn.
The honey bee so busy each and every day.
The hedgehog and her family going merrily on their way.

We give thanks to him on high, for the colours so bright,
For the pretty butterflies fluttering in the light.
This is God's gift to mankind, there is no more to say,
Except to pray and thank the Lord at the close of the day.

Jean Algar

BLACKBIRD

Blackbird, blackbird,
how joyfully you sing,
the lilting music of your song
proclaiming one more spring.

Blackbird, blackbird,
how welcome is the sound
of sweetness pouring from your throat
to mortals on the ground.

Blackbird, blackbird,
what happiness you bring
to those of us who lucky are,
to see your spreading wing.

Blackbird, blackbird,
your song will live for ever,
though winter's silence you must keep,
desert us, you will never.

Rozetta Pate

MY DREAMS

I felt you touch my cheek
In the middle of the night,
I could not see your face
But, I knew you saw me.
You wiped the tears from my eyes
And told me not to weep,
You knew what was in my heart
And said that I should sleep -
My dreams were yours to give me
And mine alone to keep.

I knew one day that we would meet
When upon the hill I'd walk -
To knock upon the door that would open
And you would let me in.
To see you waiting there -
With outstretched arms.
Then in your warm embrace
No more to feel pain or sorrow.

To walk through the Garden of Paradise
And meet with those gone long before me
Now whole and well -
Not as they were when they left
When you called them to your side
Safely to your arms,
Now young once more.
How glad am I that I knew
You would go before me
And greet me at the door
When my dreams were yours to give me
And mine alone to keep.

J O Peart

NOT A SUBSTITUTE

An old man sits in his chair,
Wondering why no one is there.
He can hear the children playing outside,
The childhood fun that he was denied.
He had to work hard for his dad,
As only little money they had.
Now all he does is sit in his chair and think,
With a bottle of whisky by his side to drink.
His bottle is the only company that he can expect,
Although it is the substitute that he should reject.
His house is covered in memories of sadness,
He reaches for his bottle but that only brings madness.
He's nothing to live for,
So he drinks more and more.
No one cares,
No one dares.
As his alcoholic addiction,
Causes neighbourhood friction.
People think he's mad,
But he's lonely and sad.
Deep down he has a warm heart,
It's been there since the start.
From the hard childhood he had,
He learnt to hide it from his dad.
When his life comes to its end.
He will not have one friend
That'll even care,
That he is no longer there.

Hannah Robertson (13)

LIVING LIFE

We all come to be born
And live our childhood.
Some may be bad,
Some may be good.
Some of us may complete our ambitions
And some of us won't.
Some of us live to die
And some of us don't.
So go ahead
And complete your dreams
That's all we have left
Or so it may seem.

Rosie Briercliffe

THINGS TO REMEMBER

Things to remember for when I go blind;
My sight will dim and to this fact I must become resigned;
It isn't people's faces that my memory longs to keep,
But the ingredients of description, sown now to later reap;
I must remember colours so that companions can describe,
The things they see before them, after my eyes have died;
White is snow, yellow is smiles, pink is candy floss,
Blue is the shiver of cold and ice, green is grass and deep cool moss;
Red is anger and heat and passion;
I need these tools so that my mind can fashion,
The pictures that my eyes can't see,
So even though I have no sight, within my mind I'll still be free.

Lynne Calvert

MOTHER

We have a loving Mother
She's very kind you see
And if you call at our house
She will order you some tea.
She sits there in her chair
And orders us about
For you see our dear old Mother
Is unable to walk about
She sits there with her Bible
Or her knitting on her knee
With a heart that's full of love
She has a face that's full of glee
Our brother he will tease her
She will hit him with her stick
For allow her legs are slow to move
Her hands are very quick
We love the way she natters
To everyone that calls
To us she's really special
We are glad she's loved by all.

Jean McLaughlin

UNTITLED

I whispered I love you and gave it to the breeze,
So you'll hear me as you walk through your life of rustling leaves,
I will hold you throughout every storm
As the trees tremble and the sea foams,
So close so safe whilst you witness the love I moaned.
When the air is still with each breath you consume you will feel me inside.
As you slowly, capture, the words of love I cried.

Karen Hartley

WAITING WITH HOPE

Like raging bulls we charged through our lives
Pulling each other along,
And when we got lost we paused for a while
To see where the road had gone.

Racing along, time flew by
Not noticing the world at all,
We only gazed forward, too scared to look back
Incase tiredness made us fall.

Then one day it tapped at your heels
Stumbling you tried to get up,
But the more you slowed down the more it grabbed hold
In the end you had to give up.

I strode on, unaware of the fact
Thinking all was right,
Though soon I did notice you lagging behind
And that's when my day became night.

You'd grown tired and weary, devoid of all feelings
Whilst I had galloped along,
I wish now I had seen it sooner
And known where we had gone wrong.

Today I sit watching the world race by
Will our roads collide?
This question flickers through my mind too much
While my loneliness I try to hide.

Michelle Carnall

FORBIDDEN FRUIT

I see the way you look at me
Sensing sensuality
But understand I am not free
To give you what you need from me.

I am a sweet forbidden fruit
You must not crave to taste
My juices flow from solid roots
My flesh with honey laced

Ripened to full maturity
My heady scent attracts you
Skin so soft and peachy peach
I cast my spell upon you

You wish to penetrate my core
Savouring each luscious bite
To pluck my leaves and leave me bare
Such is your appetite

If I should feed your heart's desire
And satiate your greed
Digested by your passion's fire
On honeyed flesh you'd feed

So gaze upon this fruit unbruised
Then walk away and leave me be
For I would weep to be so used
When you have done with me.

Maureen A Scott

THE EYES HAVE IT

My eyes have had a love affair
With you for many years
They shine when you are near me
When you go they fill with tears

It's just my eyes in love with you
Not me, you understand
'Cos I belong to someone else
There's a ring on my left hand

I told my eyes it's OK to love you
Keep it to ourselves, be smart
But have my eyes deceived me
And gone and told my heart

Now things seem rather different
They're getting rather hectic
Everytime your eyes meet mine
The feeling's quite electric!

My eyes are having trouble
Ignoring your eyes passes
So that is why I'm here today
in these dark glasses

I can't resist, my willpower's gone
You've really blown my mind
Let's go somewhere to be alone
Who cares if we go blind!

Dianne Dickinson

THE FOUR SEASONS

Daffodils and tulips, popping up everywhere.
Makes you think and feel that spring is in the air.
After spring, comes another season.
Summer is a busy time I know.
Making plans for a holiday, and just where to go.
Suddenly it is autumn, nights get darker too.
The trees start changing colour, and the skies are grey instead of blue.
You know soon it will be winter, and it is getting colder too,
Taking the seasons one by one.
I love them all you see.
Because spring, summer, autumn and the winter,
Will always be there for me.

Esme Egginton

HUMPBACK

Their backs arched high, they sail the sea
They look so huge to you and me
The waters flow the droplets fly
Another surge . . . and she's gone by.

So gentle kind and yet so sad
I wonder if she thinks she's bad

'Why else would we be pursued?
Hunted wounded misconstrued
Catch my eye you will see the fear
Is my death getting near?
I fear for my life my babies' too
Why do you humans act like you do?'

They are the angels of the sea
Watching over you and me
So why do we hurt them do them wrong
When their only crime is to sing their song.

C Robinson

THE BEACH AT WHITE ROCKS

Deserted beach bathed pale in winter light,
Metallic stretch of ocean, spiteful bite
Of wind against my cheek and plaintive cry
Of seagulls swooping in the leaden sky.
Down, down they plunge, those feathered missiles, sleek
Against the darkened shadows of the bleak

Horizon.

Here I belong, amidst the beaten rock and tufted sand
Of hills that swell like breasts before the land
That lies behind them.

Yet I must turn my steps upon the pebbled way
That leads to crumbling paths that wind along
The cliff above and in my ears the song
Of sea grows stronger.

And I must leave until the sharper gusts of winter rise to greet
The softer touch of spring and seasons meet

In celebration.

Charmian McClure

FOR THE SAKE OF THE CHILDREN

A child stands alone In the midst of a battle
His parents lost in the war
He stands and looks at the ruins around him
As more and more mortars they roar

I know it's not easy to solve people's problems
I don't know if we can end their pain
But I know we must try for the sake of that child
Before any more innocents are maimed.

Let us break down the barriers of silence
That have grown between brothers and friends
Let us break down the barriers of anger
Till all wars are at an end

Let us break down the barriers of hatred
And find out what's going wrong
Let's get people talking together
As a world we must grow strong.

Melvin Kinsey

MAXI'S LIGHT

Unlike the candle by my bed
Unlike the leaves that fall down dead
Unlike the days that change to dark
Unlike chained gates that front a park
But flowing water endlessly
Forever full forever free
Oceans blue and pastures green
Of all the beauty we have seen
Of stars that make the dark turn light
Of all the moons that shine for night
Of rain and wind and sleet and snow
A place always where roses grow
Not a day of thoughts, nor hour, nor minute
Pass me by without you in it.
And while you sleep within your dreams
When your fears turn into screams
Turn to me your candle bright
To guide you through and give you sight
Your fears will gently ease away
To dream until the light of day.

Rosemaris Jesson

THE WOODS

Walking in the woods,
Stop think and stare,
Marvel at the lovely trees
Around everywhere.

Oak elm silver birch,
Stand so tall and fair.
Glimpses of the blue sky,
Shafts of sunlight floating by.

Ferns and bushes on the ground,
Along the many paths.
Drink in their utmost.
Light from heavens above.

Birds and squirrels darting by,
Wary of man and beast.
Flying and scuttling up the trees,
With the merest breeze.

Frantic barking by the dogs,
Unable to get near.
Safety in the trees,
Residents nothing to fear.

Ancient woods, just carry on
Seasons come and go
'Oh what', tales they could tell.
Of times so long ago.

Una Woodward

WHY

Suddenly my world has changed,
Shall I tell you what I see.
The birds aren't singing anymore,
and there's dust coming down on me.

There's something wrong, there's something wrong,
I know this night shouldn't be so long.
Where is the day, where is the dawn,
Can't here the cry of life's new born.

What have we done I ask myself,
as I look all around,
For there's nothing left for anyone,
not even underground.

We won the war, with the final score,
and it seems I got the prize.
But who could see that it would be
that I'm the last one left alive.

I'm trying to keep my consciousness
but I feel I'm slipping away.
And if this is also the end for me
then I would that I could pray.

Nick Dunphy

OLD AGE

Memories are fading,
grey hairs invading,
wrinkles appearing,
the end is now nearing.

The last stage of life.
Is it empty or full?
Is life still exciting,
or gone to a lull?

Brighten up your daily hours,
let sunshine through your rainy showers.
Remember the good things, forget the bad,
try to be happy, not to be sad.

It is for your own good,
I am telling you this,
for life comes but once,
grab hold or you'll miss.

Lift up your heart,
raise it up high,
think what fun you can have,
for tomorrow, you may die.

C A Grant

THE DEVIL OF THE FOREST

He flew through the woods,
Like an eagle flying high,
A tremendous thing.

He licked at the trees,
Until they were black and burnt,
And cackled and spat.

A barn owl hooted,
As his tree disintegrated,
Eaten by the devil.

He came to a stream.
And loudly hissed,
Struggling in vain.

The animals watched,
With endless joy as he died,
The fire was no more.

Tessa Amos (13)

TRUST

People earn money,
They say it's a must,
but what's more important?
Money or trust?
You leave children in care,
you need to rely,
That they keep them safe.
You trust them, but why?
It's a chance you take,
an agreement on must,
if you break the promise,
then you've lost that trust.

Suzy Allen

GENISIS

The currants zig-zag across the bay
And out to the open sea;
The rocks drop gently into the blue
Of the shimmering waters; which seem to pursue
A distance they can never quite reach,
Stretching far out into eternity.
It's a seemingly endless void,
With an insight of sublimity
To upset our notions of self-security,
As when immersed within worldly razzmatazz
We depend too much on its humanity,
Forgetting values which are here displayed
As we endlessly, reverently, gaze and gaze
Straight into life's primordial haze.
Can we read the message it hopes to impart
Yes, the response churns within our hearts;
For here there's no sense of insecurity
But the sureness and peace of eternity
Out-lasting the lengths of transient time,
And, as durable in its purity
As is the rebirth of the creative dawn
From which generative life began.

Renée Duckworth

IN AUTUMN

Year's flowers fade and shed their blazons -
petals on the earth.
Sunsets, banking fires, invade
The smoking west;
The neon moonlight startles to delight,
And last birds singing
Carry a bequest.

At morning tide, in casual procession, cumber cows,
Loose-jointed swing endowing river's bank
With heightened colour
From each sun-bright back and steaming flank;
And , baa-ing opposite, sheep browse,
Their grey-white fleece half-buried
In the glinting green.

In ochre fields bold pheasants stately stalk,
And down the lane, road-running, partridge walk;
Slate-sheened, a heron poses;
Swans, widely white, beat bright on opal sky;
Geese arrow high, remote in flight;
And under, ducks, disturbed, noisily alight, re-float;
And the brazening sun flushes new roses.

And little-minded though our worldly minds,
Leaf-rattled autumn touches them and binds
Awareness of a conscious sort
To what we once, less-conscious, thought:
Those conjured there - now gone - we raise again;
Their precious days and bright excite anew
E'er night and winter blinds.

Mo Heenan

SANCTUARY

I am the heart of this village,
safe as the oblivion of sleep.
Seek here your peace of mind,
wrapped in the worn velvet interior,
sturdy stone keeping the enemy at bay.
Quiet, hushed, a refuge
to soothe your fretful mind.

I am here, have been here, will be here,
ashes to ashes, dust to dust.
Not a testimony to the glory of God,
but a witness to man's eternal need
for a safe-house, a haven,
where the outside world is muted.
I offer you sanctuary.

Sue Beckwith

FOREVER NEVER

A man sleeps alone.
Is it not through choice.
Could he have a partner,
Not through choice alone,
But not alone from thought.
Does this man seek solitude.
Does he seek independence.
But to see through his eyes,
So distant and glazed.
Could this be my father.
Has he come to understanding,
Or are we still to grow apart.
A choice we make together,
As we never live forever.

S M Page

THE SIMPLE JOYS OF LIFE

I awake in the morning like many days.
Opening the curtains and admiring the sun and its golden rays.

I stroll through the open fields, the leaves on the trees look so new and bright.
Several birds are gathered, about to embark on their daily plight.

I arrive at the beach, the sea looks so calm and serene,
The reflection of the bright blue sky, gives the rippling waves a glorious sheen.

I feel the fresh sea breeze, against my glowing skin.
Suddenly I realise that to never have come here, would have been a real sin.

I feel a sense of satisfaction as the day has passed.
So many wonderful things to see and do, oh why must time go so fast.

Darkness has fallen, and the moon is now in sight.
So beautiful and shimmering, now I know it is time to say goodnight.

T J Neale

DAYBREAK

Daybreak . . .
The silver light of dawn
Intrudes
Upon my sleeping form
As like a butterfly
Leaving his cocoon,
A babe
Emerging from the womb,
I embrace each day
A pristine page
In my unwritten history.

Avril Seatter

DAWN CHORUS

The blackbird in the oak tree sings his heart
out to his mate,
The spring has come, 'let's build our nest, before
it is too late.
The speckled thrush with joyous heart, sings
from the top most bough.
'Come my love the winter's gone, and it is
springtime now,'
The cheeky robin, with breast so red, chirps as
he works away,
The sparrows, too, join in the song for it is
break of day,
The rook, upon the chimney tall, gives out his
raucous cry
The seagull, on his outspread wings, squawks as
he glides by.
Every bird, it seems, gives note on branch or on
the wing.
The world pulsates with joyful sound, to herald
in the spring.
Each dawn the air is full of sound and rouses me
from sleep.
Then, off they fly, to start their day, as 'neath
the clothes I creep.
Some people love bird song at dawn, this I will
allow.
But it is just 5.30, must they make that dreadful
row!

D E Stalton

A HAPPY NEW YEAR

In January it's time to make
Our New Year resolutions.
To put aside our former cares
And to provide solutions.

To cut the booze, to quit the fags
And tackle every chore.
Get on with our relations
Including Mother-in-law.

The TV will take second place
Computers even less
To give up playing all those games
Is hard I must confess.

But there are more important things
And jobs that must be done.
Some DIY around the house
Can really be quite fun.

To think of all those tasks completed
Just like them next door
New windows doors and patio
And brand new wood block floor.

That's why we like 'the Good Old Days'
When lots of us were poor.
Instead of sacrificing things
We simply hoped for more.

Chris Phillips

THEN

Everything was better then.
Colours were brighter then.
The rooms in my house were bigger then.
Snow was whiter then.

'Trick or treat' was great fun then.
Autumn and winter were colder then.
'Behave' was often said to you then.
Teachers were older then.

Jam sandwiches were tasty then.
Building dens under tables was magical then.
'The Ten o'clock News' was never seen then.
The death of a goldfish was tragical then.

Summer holidays lasted for ever then.
Bottoms would fit into playground swings then.
The garden was enormous and marvellous then,
I didn't mind picking up worms and things then.

Birthdays brought more presents then.
Grandad was bigger and hairier then.
Parents had answers to everything then.
The airing cupboard was scarier then.

Life was unlimited and unknown then.
Friendships did not need to last then.
Family was taken for granted then.
I did not think of the future or the past then.

Richard Hughes

SUMMER

Have you seen the sky so blue,
A hint of dampness from the dew,
The skylark singing up on high,
And swallows swirling in the sky,
The fields of golden ripening corn
With swathes of poppies to adorn,
Their scarlet tissue paper flowers
Brighten up our summer hours.
And combine harvesters drone away
In fields of barley, wheat and hay,
The sun is high and days are warm,
The farmers work afeared of storms,
The bees are busy every hour
Visiting the many fragrant flowers,
Grass hoppers chirp in the grass,
The cool clear stream goes gurgling past,
A place to quench for bird and beast
As sweet as nectar at a feast,
And minnows darting in the shallows
Taking shelter in the shadows
Stalking tiny insect swimmers
Hungry for their needed dinners.
The trees stand quietly in the heat
Their mantle of leaves giving shade at their feet,
A busy time for everyone
Ruled by the seasonal summer sun.

Yvonne Holmes

YOU AND I

As you stand, tired, expressionless
I can see through the blankness
I know you. I know what you are feeling.
But from the depths you breathe, and start again.
A new query, another demand
And yet the answers, so wise, never cease.
We say we love you,
God says 'Actions speak louder than words.'
So why don't we show you more often?
I demand.
I am selfish.
I am.
You give.
You are resentless.
You are my mother.
Love is unconditional, but you are not love.
You are merely human.
In your weakness I am given strength.
That is *my* action - to be strong.
And so, I love you.

Patricia McCafferty

BY-PASS

There's a peace here,
Beneath the blue-green speckling of
The forest canopy;
There's a stream that flows,
It's the loudest noise I know,
And I feel human,
Soon they will erase this scene,
Only to know it in our dreams,

For here they will build
Yet another road,
To by-pass the town,
And join with the road,
Which leads to the road,
Which goes to the road,
Which leads to the road,
Which goes to nowhere.

John Watson

WHY?

Why did he betray me?
Why doesn't he care?
Doesn't he know how much it hurts
To be met by that crushing stare?
I thought you'd always be there.
You promised, but you lied.
And now I have no-one to love
And fill this empty void.
My emotions lie in pieces,
For you they once were strong,
My heart's a painful memory
Of how you did me wrong.
You've left me with no dignity.
I'm dirt beneath your shoe.
But you were the one who mislead *me*
The bad guy should be you.
I loved you, now I cannot rest.
My body aches with grief.
So I'm to leave this harsh world now,
My death will be relief.

Diana Best

THE RIVER

Feet tickling languid shallows,
river weed trailing from rounded rocks;
minnows meandering,
as a small child's net
encapsulates entwining eels.

Babbling white water
fringed with foam,
frothing furiously into dark backwaters
which murkily, muddily
belch wonderful white waterfalls;
see them cascade
in a wonderful cacophony;
rainbow rimmed and resplendent
as they vanish
into a silent pool below.

Julia Bain

VISION

I've waited and waited and still it doesn't come,
How long is everlasting for it must seem to some,
The time isn't yet right,
The end still far away,
Yet still the impatience does not go away.
It moulds and it shapes your life yet to come,
For who knows its secret the mysterious one,
Changes do happen of a world turning kind,
For some disaster for others, 'never mind',
What the eyes see from one, the mind in another,
affected, and reflected,
What means to one means nothing to another.

Lindsay McCaffery

THE AWAKENING

The light of dawn begins to break and spread across the sky
Then all the little birds awake, singing sweetly as they fly.
And suddenly I'm wakened too, back to reality again
For in my dream I was with you, as fast asleep I'd lain.

A vivid dream so real and true, a split second and it fades
So do I blame the cuckoo, who now my peace invades?
Somewhere hidden in a tree, he sings his plaintiff song
But does he know he's saddened me, that now my dream is gone?

And as I lie there and listen, sweet warbles fill the air
Outside the roses glisten from the dew that has been there
The Earth smells sweet and fragrant, a glorious summer day
There's only one thing missing, you are now far away

But hopefully the time will pass, through hurried night and day
Until at last the moment comes, when you are on your way.
Then will the morning's beauty, in all its splendour show
As the warmth that builds inside me, becomes an outward glow.

P D Fuller

PATIENCE

A mind within that crumpled shell
A heart that's steady beating,
A soul that's pure as driven snow
A courage takes some beating
What makes her smile, we've got to know
But patience, love, will prove
It might take days,
It might take weeks,
But even mountains move.

Lilian Summers

REFLECTING

If I should ever die,
as life slips away,
I would pause to wonder why,
or how, I never said
so many words I want to say.

Oh, that my heart could tell
the depth of love . . .
feelings so much like a spell . . .
many words I have wanted to speak
and yet . . . they sound so *weak.*

How can I explain my all?
The very being of my heart?
No words can suffice . . .
these feelings will remain
forever - lest we part.

One thing I have to say
and remains so very true . . .
I feel at one in every way
so much a part of you.

Georgina Skinner

EVACUEE

Evacuee, evacuee all he sees is a sea of hands,
that disappear in all the smoke.
A tear from each eye comes rolling down
his face. What can he see, all on his own,
scared, alone, upset, feeling unwanted.

Coming off the train lots of people
pushing and pulling at each and every child.
He hears planes flying overhead,
people scream and shout, running for their lives.

Then all he hears is a very loud bang.
Silence falls.
All he can see is a misty graveyard of people.

Christian Chalfont

ONE OF THOSE NIGHTS

One of those nights,
When I can't get to sleep,
The prison so quiet,
I can't hear a peep.

One of those nights,
Where I toss and I turn,
The prison so quiet,
'Tis morning I yearn.

One of those nights,
Where in darkness I stare,
The prison so quiet,
As I lay in my lair.

One of those nights,
Where I just seem to blink,
The prison so quiet,
I can only but think.

One of those nights,
I wish it would end,
The prison so quiet,
I'm glad I'm my friend.

Sonny E Duncombe

THE INTRUDER

(Solitude of the heart)

Solitude . . .
Our inconsiderate co-partner -
Constantly in ambush . . .
Uninvited,
Heedless of our discordant self.
Inconsolable . . .
Deaf to all our voiceless protestations.

Solitude -
A sore peril to those nearby . . .
Contagious?
Something to avoid.
We may not comprehend
If enemy or friend?

Insatiable -
Gnawing at our very roots . . .
As difficult to disentangle
As clinging as the ivy to the tree
To which it even might embellish!

Belinda Del Re

THE LONG YEAR

A baby cries in the early morning.
An unseen hand on a virgin page leaves its mark.
A new awakening; a New Year dawning.
The spring of life is announced by a lark.

Like a leggy fawn, the child grows
with each day a new awareness; and buds open into flowers.
Games are played and the laughter flows.
The summer of life with its carefree hours.

A wedding embraces another season
as the lovers continue along life's leafy glade.
The arrival of children gives love more reason.
The autumn of life, and the blooms start to fade.

The scattered petals of the red, red rose
are the pains of old age though the heart is still brave.
A last breath is taken as the book covers close.
The winter of life in the arms of the grave.

Joy Richards

WHAT IS IT ALL FOR?

Life, what is it all about?
We study hard, for the results we want, we strive so hard
to achieve our ambition, but when we reach our ambition
then what?
We go through a lot, protesting for our rights, fighting for
things we want, but then we win and receive what
we want, then what?
We think we've found the right person in our lives, someone
we can love and cherish forever, but when they break our
hearts, then what?
We fall in love, then have a broken heart, what is it all for?
We make friends and have a family, but when we die and
leave our loved ones, then what?
We achieve so much throughout our lives with continuous
effort, what is it all for?
We earn respect and gain love, but what is it all for?
It all just ends in one minute, what do we achieve then?

Rehana Choudhury (15)

LONELY TIMES

Where loneliness exists,
Night-time need not;
The dark and the silence,
Are never forgot.

An hour goes on,
Forever or more;
Amazing the thoughts,
Your mind will explore.

When an idea arises,
No ears to fall on;
An answer's awaited,
No mouth to come from.

The silence gets louder,
It won't quieten down;
There to remind you,
You're there on your own.

But faith is the answer,
And dreams aren't a crime;
Comfort will come,
With courage and time.

Karen Ann Rigg

MYSELF

Gemini lady hard to catch
Gemini lady - weary to watch
Gemini lady - won't you please stop!
Always trying to beat the clock.

Full of talent, ideas over flow
No patience whatever with folk who are slow
She needs all the eyes of a spider to use
All the limbs of an octopus she can use too
For all the things she plans to do
Six jobs are not too many for her
Two is not enough I fear
Just like a butterfly flitting around
Or onto the sun-shine covering ground

'Oh why can't we live without sleep' she cries
While she vainly struggles to prop open her eyes!
Gemini ladies are people apart
When old in years - still young at heart
Lovers of nature and sweet solitude
Of wide open spaces and deep old woods
With many old trees where birds fly around
And carpets of violets cover the ground.

A good night's sleep? - People die in bed!
Time is awasting is what she said
'Relax?' they say - 'well not today!'
Can't change the Gemini lady!

Ruth Burden

FIRST TO LAST

My cheeks blushing
My pulse racing
When you smiled at me
for the *first time.*
The anticipation flowing through my veins
When our lips met
For the *first time.*
My whole body in ecstasy
Alive and electric
When we made love
For the *first time.*
My mind in a turmoil
The pain so severe
The tears falling down
Dying inside
My heart torn in shreds
When you said goodbye
For the *last time.*

Bridget Ward

JOHN

So falls the night and we pull our shutters
On the dramattis personae of the gutters:
So falls a life
So stills a heart
So flies a secret name to its maker's bosom

We tell ourselves it's a mystery
Or he was misdealt his place in history
(Those of us who know our place
Jostling for position in this human race
running before the confused eyes of the secret one.)

So he left us
Took his gruff manner and laugh
Walked off down the wind with the dust and the chaff
At rest now his feet
Peaceful his grave
As his maker takes back
John's secret name
That He gave.

Tony Fox

MEMORIES

When we visited a friend what a welcome we had
Just a knock on the door we knew we felt glad
The step and the knocker all shiny and bright
The smiling face what a welcome sight
Come on in let's have a cup of tea
Tell me your news and I tell you about me
The lively open fire piled with coal and logs
To keep out the cold and nasty old fog
Curtains were never drawn at night
Paraffin lamps all lively and bright
What do we have now gas fires central heating too
Curtains now pulled windows made secure
Doors bolted and locked is what we endure
Just to be safe from muggings murder and lies
We try and remember the years gone by.
They say that progress is the name of the game
To us older folk the world will never be the same
To keep your friends and be careful when you meet
For your cup of tea and a cake for a treat
So as you say cheerio my friend
Don't forget lock up be safe it helps
no end.

Patsy Pope

FAIR SHARES?

Lots for you and little for me,
This is very plain to see,
You get choice on what you eat,
Cheese, bread, cakes and meat,
All we get is a little rice,
Which isn't filling and not very nice.
But it's all we have to eat,
A little bread would be a treat,
You waste water all the time,
For us that would be a crime,
We hardly get to have a drink,
So why don't you just stop and think?
Think of all the things for you,
You get more - that is true,
Think of all the things for me.
There isn't very much to see,
You have peace - for me there's war,
You sit on chairs - we use the floor,
We always come second best,
You always come above the rest,
You are rich and we are poor,
And for everything - you get more.
Does justice come into this?
To live like you would be bliss,
We shouldn't have to live this way,
Scraping for food from day to day,
Will justice ever be done?
Or will you always be number one?

Rebecca Wilson (14)

UNTITLED

She had the body of a woman but the mind of a child
And she was still at school
She was young and innocent looking for love
But she didn't know his rules
He will love you and leave you her friends would say
But she wouldn't listen you see
Her feelings and emotions just got in the way
And now she just wants to be free
She mistook sex for love that she didn't get at home
She just wanted to be held near
She just wanted assurance when things were going wrong
And someone to wipe away the tear
All she could see was a family home
Not a tower-block flat where she sits on her own
At weekends when all her old friends are out
She works out the budget and just wants to shout

But she will take care of her baby
Her maternal instincts are strong
And she'll somehow survive
Even when things go wrong
She'll try to give her baby what she really needs
Like a hug and a kiss between the four-hourly feeds
But who wants a single parent the boys just want sex
And a few cans of lager to pour down their necks
But maybe she'll find him, her hero so fair
But for now she'll just stand by the window and stare.

Fred Gates

OASIS OF SANITY

When I willed myself to breath no more
weighing up all there is to exist for
I craved my heart to cease silently
faltering to doom wraiths, beckoning me
but you, my wisdom, grace and tenderness
you are my odd oasis of sanity in desolate wilderness.

Pricked the reins of time to halt for me
reasoned with suffering to let me be
you cleared the thorns that filled my path
forged my soul in heaven's respite, for hell's wrath
my prayer, my glory, merciful benevolence
you are my odd oasis of sanity in desolate wilderness.

In un-fruitful lands my soul did not thirst
like hounds from hell, others causelessly cursed
but you endeavoured to provide, by hook, by crook,
still hell came, our joys it took
my spirit, my valour, dauntlessness
you are my odd oasis of sanity in desolate wilderness.

If in your womb, I was that treasure
blessed to spurn fate, scorn fear
Through dissipating innocence I see your pain
chronicled in your eyes, burnt upon my brain.
I am your hopes, your rock, your fortress,
I am your odd oasis of sanity in desolate wilderness.

Selina Caan

STORMBREAK

So the storm breaks, just when things seem to be good,
brings savage frustration to an already fragile thought
and like a thief, it takes away the smile
soft diffusion leaves, a mark, the blameless caught.

Viscious lightning bites hard and deep to the bottom of the soul,
crazy thunder roars until nothing makes any sense,
a howling gale beats at the door of reality.
For the delicate and the gentle, there is no defence.

Driving tears boil and cascade, always on the inside,
concealing salty rain from too many prying eyes.
A primitive reply to open-hearted friendship,
crashing deceit from harmless white lies.

The mind screams in defiance, 'It doesn't matter.
Nobody won and nothing was gained, there need not be a why.'
But the ever more sensitive heart starts to bleed,
and another piece of the spirit begins to wither and die.

Only shadows survive the desolation that loneliness brings,
echoing possible reminders of how little is understood.
So the storm rages on through shattered peace
and poisonous betrayal strips away the good.

Phillip Barnes

THIS MOMENT

If I were banished to the Halls of Time
And heard the bells of all the Ages chime
Hustled back then on ten thousand years
Beyond all present thoughts and hopes and fears,
Still would this moment keep its place with me
Though I on wings sped to Eternity.

If I should see the multitudes arise
Then fade and perish there before my eyes
And feel the searing flames of love and hate -
Twin torches that the years do not abate -
Yet what I feel I still would know again
For this is safe beyond both joy and pain.

Above the babble of a million tongues
Deafened by a thousand anthems sung,
The fearsome noise of every human war
Still would I hear above the cannons' roar
That quiet voice, as in a cloistered spot
Which spoke this moment, not to be forgot.

If I were offered palaces of kings
With power over all insensate things
To stay, to dwell in some idyllic place
Above mortality in Time and Space,
Still would my spirit to this moment true
Give all, if but it might be born anew.

Jack Crossman

GRANNY'S WRINKLES

I loved my granny's wrinkles
To me, they were divine.
I'd sit upon her soft plump lap
Enthralled by every line.

They told so many stories
You only had to look,
When I was young and couldn't read
They were my picture book.

Her life had not been easy
She'd worked hard in the mill,
And though her sight was dimming
Her eyes they sparkled still.

Framed by darkened shadows
Which sleep could not erase,
Two pale blue orbs would twinkle
And brighten all my days.

Who wants a glamorous granny
All done up to the nines?
Who's undergone a facelift
To rid herself of lines?

We love our grey-haired grannies
wrinkles, lines and all,
For beauty's only skin deep
But love comes from the soul.

Kay Leaver

THE WEATHER MAN

You stormed in like a hurricane
And turned life upside-down
You crashed in like a tidal wave
Till I thought I'd nearly drown.
You warmed my being with golden rays
That caressed my tender heart
Then sped away like a tornado
And blew my mind apart.
You relieved me like a summer rain
My thirsty soul did sate.
You embraced me like an autumn breeze
That kept me warm and safe.
Then like a harsh, cold winter frost
You chilled me to the bone.
And with the gentle thaw of spring
I found I was alone.

Lynne Morris

UNTITLED

Can it be that there is fate
A governing force that sets the pace
That nothing's premature or late
But everything is in its place

Are decisions already made
Our furrowed brows just creased in vain
Is all we say previously said
And all our sorrow carved in pain

Or do we choose a path that's new
I truly wonder if that's so
Yet maybe even if that's true
It always was the way we'd go.

G Hawkins

SERENITY

A crescent moon arose before the sun had gone.
Her light seemed pale against the reddened sky,
Her splendour muted by a brighter fire,
Her beauty lost in the glory of the sun.

Then all at once, the realm of day was overthrown,
Though silhouettes of hills could still be seen,
The trees grew strangely darker in the softer gleam,
Serenity itself hung in the night, her beauty shone alone.

The fragrant air, yet warm from summer's golden glowing,
Was still. The velvet blackness spread its calm,
Nothing was visible in this night's balm,
Except the gleaming silver crescent moon, now all her
radiance showing.

Linda Leach

I WISH

I wish that I could write a poem that everyone admired
It would be published in the best of books,
Something to be desired.
I wish that I could write a song that everyone could sing
It would be in all the record shops
Along with Frank and Bing.
I wish that I dare tell you, what you mean to me
I would say how much I loved you
And hope that you loved me.
I wish I could stop wishing
It would be perfect bliss
But to make this world a better place
I'll just have one more wish.

T Hannah

BEAUTIFUL SPRING

Bud break at last!
The long, cold fast of winter
Is broken;
Renewal has begun;
Warmed by the light
Of the glorious sun,
While the warm sou' westerly breeze,
Gently rocks the trees
And shimmies the leaves
Of the still clad evergreen bushes.
Oh beautiful spring!
Herald of lighter nights,
Long days of useful activity;
Warm rain gently falling
Washing winter's grip away,
Softening the earth, and promoting,
Floral reactivity.
Blossom waxing on my trees
At the waning of the freeze
And flowers in my garden;
Little faces turned upwards to the light
To my delight.

Louisa M Stokoe

ARISE MY LOVE

Arise my love and let us go
to a far away place where we can show
our love for each other without care or fear
of wagging tongues or lips that sneer.

No more deceit, and no more lies
no more avoiding each other's eyes
lest we confirm what some suspect
(one or two already know, I expect).

A love such as ours should not be concealed
but should be, in all its beauty revealed
Beautiful it is, and as such comes to few
How wonderful that it came to me and you.

So come my love and let us go
to that far away place where we can show
to the world at large our love for each other
a love which is growing and will last forever.

G Shepherd

IT

In a tranquil; twilight tone
I find myself repeating it,
like a much loved poem
learned by heart,
framed and
mounted on my wall.

It makes me say it
quietly,
until I experience the moon's silence.
Spoken slowly it lends
clarity to its mystery.

Evoking nostalgia
it appears reassuringly old fashioned,
though it sometimes seems quite modern
and proud to be free.

It dies tragically
apparently with no forewarning,
but it is the alternative
to all we possess.

Jeff Roberts

SIGH

Up from me and out swells the deep sigh.
The breath of descent from the all time high.
The sigh, nothing more than a sound expresses,
the emptiness I feel all around.
Like the noise of a club that echoes round your empty heart.
Like leaning out of your window late at night,
with the ice of the midnight air ruffling your hair and surveying the horizon
by the amber glow of the lamp outside.
Like the parting embrace, the loosing of the hold, that I have to face.
It's like cooling down after the warmth of a hug, full of friendship,
Like sprawling in front of an open fire
while the snow floats down and puts out my desire.
Like sharing the stars with someone as you gaze at the diamonds
set into the thick blanket of night.
Like when you're with someone and all around you hear
nothing, and even the beating of your own heart stills.
Through the silence you hear the unsaid things, the
telepathy of friendship, shouts 'Being with you is all that I wanna do.'
It's that funny thing you remember, when no-one's there.
At least no-one that would get it, with whom you could share.
That causes the grin that makes others wonder.
That works the magic of the spell you're under.
The music stops, and I'm left all alone,
With my thoughts and the quiet of night
That drowns out the fight, my internal struggle.
All these things and much much more say the fading
desire that I feel - means I belong.
I belong to the club of those weak, who need someone to be strong.
And as I yearn for that something true. I realise something.
I'm a member of the club that's looking for You.

Mark Langdown

THE BLUEBELL

When autumn is over,
And winter is gone,
I rise in the spring,
To shout at the sun.

In a coat of silver,
And a coat of blue,
I sing my rude chorus,
As I bathe in the dew.

In woods of deep slumber,
I tip-toe on,
Hushed by a mist,
I dance naught'ly on.

In pots of plenty,
And vases so fine,
In children's' stories too,
I am so divine.

But as the year passes by,
Into summer's full dress,
Old age comes a creeping,
And steals my blue vest.

For now I am naked,
And my song is all spent,
So I hide under ground,
Until I repent!

Paul MacMillan

THE COLLECTOR

Flash black, and white
glides glistening
green blue
greed

bleak
gun metalled precision,
stabbing
beak

grabbing
makes his collection
strutting his stuff
conceit
protection

crouched cats
faded pride
beneath
muted acceptance of
the thief

one for sorrow,
and again,
tomorrow.

Jenny O'Brien

SUMMER

The sun is shining,
Here and there,
Flowers are just everywhere.
Everywhere the birds
Are singing,
In all the churches,
Bells are ringing.

People going to the beach,
They will take a picnic each.
The countryside is full of roses,
No-one now is sniffing their noses,
The trees are only filled
With leaves,
In some places there is a breeze.

Here and there,
There are some showers,
But they are only for the flowers.
In the country there is fresh air,
On some of the trees there is
A pear,
Winter time has gone away,
Welcome to the lovely day!

Leanne Fitzgerald (8)

MEMORIES OF YOU

If I could see you,
Just once,
it would be a dream,
this is what I feel,
it burns like a fire,
deep down inside,
my heart beats,
just for you,
my thoughts,
my dreams,
you are there,
you are in my mind,
and in my heart,
I want to cuddle you,
I want to hold you,
I can't,
when I'm sad,
you cheer me up,
all I have to do is look,
there you are in my head,
like a photo,
you're standing there smiling,
that's all I have of you,
is memories,
I'm there for you,
and you're there for me,
you keep me going,
not knowing
where we're going,
then you're gone.

Brian Harris

ESCAPE

In all of us is the need to escape
Often from our occupation
That's why each year we save, and save
Just to go on vacation.

We're escaping when we take a break
Even a day at the zoo
Look at the animals in their cages
They must want to escape too!

Sport is used for escaping
From the hustle and bustle of life
A man often goes to a football match
To escape from his trouble and strife!

Bars are put on windows
To keep criminals in their cells
If these were suddenly to vanish
Prisoners would escape as well!

Drugs and drink are escapism
Or other obnoxious acts
Taking refuge in fantasy,
To avoid disagreeable facts.

You don't have to leave the country
Or a prison, or even red tape
You just need to look around you
There are plenty of ways to escape.

E Waldron

THE SNAIL

Slithery slow snail
Secure upon the ground;
High upon your stodgy back
Your shell is fastened sound

Your eyes are held aloft
Erect upon two sticks:
Scrutinising closely
Nature's nasty tricks.

When sensitive of danger
You pull your eye-balls in
Contracting up so tightly
Your grey and sticky skin.

You leave a path behind you:
A silvery slimy slope!
Telling tales of wandering
As slowly on you grope.

Rosaleen Crossan

THE BOASTING SPIDER

Me and my kind are the scariest creatures.
We're hairy and creepy with the ugliest features.
When we're up on the ceiling no-one can reach us.
I catch flies by the dozen,
Once I've caught 'em,
They stop buzzin'.

Jessica Williams (10)

I CAN SEE . . .

When I look out the window what do I see?
Not a garden of flowers, not even a tree.

I can see big chimneys pouring out smoke,
I can see a main road, car fumes making us choke.

I cannot see green grass, roses of red,
I can see noisy traffic, plants that are dead.

What do I see when I walk down the road?
A canal full of rubbish my eyes do behold.

The water is gloomy, the fishes are dead,
Maybe a shopping trolley fell on their head.

With everybody's rubbish the water's full to the brim,
The sign says '*No bathing*' - there's *no room* to swim!

Kerry Louise Till (15)

UNTITLED

I wish I was alive
Oh how I wish,
I was alive,
When I drift, down the street
see the people pass me by,
I wish I could grasp, and caress you
I wish I was alive.

I could kiss the ladies
and shake a man's hand.
I would give you the pennies
from my pocket.
How I wish I was alive.
Give me hope, Lord, a new prayer
I know, you're more than alive.

Brian Hair

HERE

Incredibly, you're still here
Golden lights in your hair
Glowing like fire
Your power.
The constable day
Worrying clouds on a thin horizon
Like the thoughts in the front of your head
That hover out of needs not met.
You give
And the day is fierce with colour.
Time's breath has beaten
Like rain on the window
Yet you rise like a mountain
out of the sea.
I have closed my eyes, I have
closed my eyes
But incredibly you're still here.

Heather Freckleton

TEMPTED

Now then Mum, you shouldn't buy it,
you know you're sticking to that diet.
It looks inviting, sweet and sticky,
sat on the shelf there, looking pretty,
calling to you, 'Buy me buy me,'
'You'll get one free, if you just try me.'
Taking over your mind and senses,
knocking down all your defences.
Take a deep breath and push it aside,
consult your pocket calorie guide.
Don't do it Mum, don't let it win,
If you eat that cake, you won't get thin!

Debbie Leatherdale

OUR LOVE

With the first sight of you, my love began to grow.
I could not feel, I could not know.
And through my eyes, I could not see,
Your beautiful face, so full of misery.

The silent tears, you need to shed,
Memories of pain going through your head.
But something in my heart just blew,
And all I wanted was to be with you.

My strong loving arms brought you comfort,
No longer would your heartaches hurt.
Watching over you. every waking hour,
Doing everything for you, within my power.

With every breath, I hope and pray,
Our love will grow stronger each day.
A special bond will bring us together,
And make our love, last forever.

Dee-Ann Cronshaw

BUTTON-HOLED

It looks like the computer
is almost here to stay,
It puts thousands of people
out of work every single day,
We talk about education
and the levels that are met,
There will soon be no education,
It will all be internet,
With the press of a button,
To the dole office we are sent,
The only ones left in work,
Are our wonderful Government!

Dennis

HIDING PRESENTS

They've done it again,
They've had a look,
The Christmas presents have all been shook,
The wardrobe's open,
They've been scrutinised,
And told the others,
There's no surprise.

I caught one coming out my room,
I know what they've seen,
I'm full of gloom,
I've told them they're for somebody else,
They smiled and said 'Are they for yourself.'

I'm angry that there's no space to hide,
The Christmas gifts I bought with pride,
Those little monsters have spoilt it all,
But they can't wait for Christmas to fall,

I love them dearly,
I did this when I was young,
I do declare, it was full of fun.

J B Kelly

SUSPENSE

There you are waiting for an outcome,
Wondering if it will be good,
You hope in your heart it's a winner,
And if you think so, maybe they should.

You're wandering around in dreamland,
Nothing you do is correct,
Because you're worrying over the outcome,
As your future you're trying to erect.

The suspense is truly overwhelming,
Your nerves they are tight and taught,
Sometimes you wish you'd never been born,
As in one of life's traps you are caught.

Please tell me I can't wait any longer,
Your thoughts are eating me away,
Please make this a day to remember,
Please make it my good news day.

B A Jones

ONCE 2 OFTEN

You broke my heart
and that's so true
but then I was a fool
to give it to you.

You made me cry
nearly every day
and just when I was on the mend
you took your love away.

I cried and cried
but what good was that
I wish you here beside me
but still alone I sit and have sat.

I wanted your love
for my soul to feed
I didn't give you my heart
to make it bleed.

I needed your love
on so many days
but now my heart is broken
in oh so many ways.

Charlene Whelan

HIGH ON THE HILL

Stop the clock
And make time stand still
Slow down the breeze
High on the hill
Freeze the sun in the sky
Put the cloud on hold
Don't let bring the night
Don't let it grow too cold

Stop the rain
Let the river be still
Let it be quiet
High on the hill
Let the trees grow high
As long as they don't move
I don't really know why
But this is what I choose

Stop the moment there
While she is undressed
Touch the silkiness of her hair
So beautiful in a mess
I remember making love
And praying for time to stand still
'Cause I know I couldn't get enough
High on the hill.

Barry Towers

DAISY CHAIN

(A poem to my Granddaughter)

When I was very little,
Playing in a field,
I picked some little daisies,
To make a daisy chain,
I arranged them very carefully,
To put upon my head,
When I had finished doing that,
I felt like a little princess,
I had some daisies over,
So I made a little bracelet.

Gwen Lloyd

FAT LADY

It's hard to let go of that final last link
To reach 50 and realise a size 16 is not slink
Slimming and starving I've tried them all
It just seems I'm growing more into a ball
Two stone is my goal to try and loose
At the moment I am more likely to snooze
This diet is making me so tired
Now three weeks has past I think I will hire
Someone to put a tuck in my spare tyre
2 oz less cannot possibly be right
I crave for a choccy bar especially at night
There's only one answer to my plight I can see
Short of cutting off my legs at the knees
As a Nanny I will have to be
Round and cuddly, blow the diet, let's have tea!

Sonia Howes

THE DAY, THE MATCH, THE DISAPPOINTMENT

Off to the match on a weeks' Saturday,
Expecting the best of the game on display,
On to the terraces crowding together,
Does not matter what type of weather,
Wind, rain, snow and sleet,
We're here to see the teams compete.

Chanting the slogans, singing the songs,
Hoping our team doesn't go wrong,
Kick off's at three, there's five minutes to go,
Singing, chanting, swaying two and fro,
Bubbling excitement now fills the air,
The fans know the teams will soon be out there,

But just a minute? The Ref's coming out,
He's on to the field, he's stamping about?
Now he is going back off the field,
The Tannoy crackles, what will it yield,
Oh! The match is called off because of the frost,
And as per usual it's the fans that have lost.
'Oh! Pure disappointment'

Reginald Dutton

FLING BACK THE CURTAIN!

Fling back the curtain and let the light in!
The night-time is over - the day shall begin.
No need to remember the tears of the night
Open the window - this day will be bright!

In sorrow we lay in a darkened room
The hours were long and heavy the gloom.
Yet in the stillness a peacefulness creeps
And rest soothes the mind and thankfully sleeps.

So now is the morning and time to arise
Time to take action and open the eyes
Fling back the curtain and look at the scene
As the gold of autumn changes a summer of green.

Don't hesitate to fearlessly gaze
On a world of problems lost in a maze
You might be one to heal the pain
So others may open their windows again.

Anne P Crowther

SHADOWS

I saw her once again today,
So alive and free,
Running, jumping, way up high,
From the ground,
Up to the sky,
Lithe and graceful with such ease,
Has no cares,
Herself to please,
Like a river twisting and bending
Her love of life is never-ending,
Like a child,
She flits and flees,
Here and there, upon the breeze,
Then at night she goes away,
To return some other day,
Then I look close, and I see,
That the shadow dance is me.

Patricia A Robinson

IT'S NOT MY FAULT IF I'VE GOT FLEAS!

They treat me as if I'm an alien
'Don't touch him, he's got them,' they shout
I circle their legs till I'm dizzy
They cringe and then throw me out.

They say, 'Take your fleas round to Margaret's.'
Or, 'Get lost and go hunt for some mice!'
How dare they when they're just as dirty
It's not my fault if I have some lice.

I do what I can to avoid them
I wash twice a day, even more,
I choke all the time on my hair balls
I lick till my tongue becomes sore.

They think they're the ones with the problem
'He's a filthy old moggy,' they say
I don't get the cuddles I used to
They don't get the string out to play.

But I am the one with the itches
I have to go through the pain,
Then in all my anguish and suffering
They throw me outside in the rain.

But the worst thing of all are the lotions
The collars, the sprays and the cream,
They put me through hours of torture
If only all this was a dream.

Debbie Glover (14)

NOTHING CAN DESTROY YOUR SOUL

There are many things in our complex lives,
We often take for granted.
Everything we have today,
Our existence, nature planted.

All sorts of unexpected happenings,
Are often sent our way.
None of them as punishment,
But to keep our souls at bay.

No matter what you have been dealt,
Throughout your own existence.
It is for you to carry on,
Regardless of the instance.

Remember when you sow the seeds,
Patience provides the power,
Firstly roots and then the shoots,
Producing a scented flower.

Remember the overwhelming pureness,
Of the unblemished baby's hand.
The gentleness of his tiny breath,
Silken threads of each hair strand.

Remember what it means to have,
The pleasures of a smile.
Laughter ringing in your ears,
Facial creases stay a while.

So always when you're in distress,
And hope's completely lost.
Nothing can destroy your soul,
No matter what the cost.

Sam Cato

A NEW BEGINNING

And now that you've passed over,
To a land where dreams come true.
Where love grows ever stronger,
I wish to be with you.

Show me where I can pass over,
To the gates of this far off land.
So that I may see its beauty,
So that I may understand.

Take my hand, lead me closer,
Let me breathe in the air.
Let me feel all those feelings,
I wish to be there.

Let me see all the colours,
Let me hear all the sounds.
Let me come and fly with you,
I wish not to be Earthbound.

But I know I can't pass over,
To the land where dreams come true.
To a place where love's forever,
I cannot be with you.

Now that you have left me,
For a place far away.
I understand the reason,
I'll see you there someday.

Vickey Bagg

A DOLPHIN'S LIFE

Gliding through the water he goes
What's in his future - nobody knows.

A poacher waiting, with spear in his hand,
He strikes at the creature, and sadness roams
his deep sea hands

A wave of his fin, a sparkle in his eyes
With a trickle of blood, he slowly dies . . .

Hilary Webb (14)

ODE TO A BUBBLE

Air through water flows
Forms a bubble that goes
Merrily, merrily along.

A beautiful lustrous globe
in which muted lights strobe,
Rainbows shine and dance
Reflections gleam perchance
dreams, encapsulated drift.

Unfulfilled wishes lift
upwards; you are a magic moment
Alive! Irradiating joy.

Your mirrored surface,
lovelier than any jewel,
shines and glows, wobbling,
a translucent jelly
caught in a perfect sphere
till popped! You disappear.

Elizabeth Davies

THE WINDS OF CHANGE

Someone has stood beside us
As we've grown throughout the years,
Through the happiness and sadness
Of our first loves, and our first tears.

When problems we've encountered,
You've been our guiding light,
A beacon throughout the stormy days,
And through the darkest nights.

Our childhood now is in the past,
Those wonderful days are gone,
But those special years that we treasured
In our minds will still live on.

We've all grown that much older now,
And the winds of change have blown.
You know that you can lean on us,
That you'll never stand alone.

As you were always there for us,
To dispel our darkest fears,
So we will always be there for you,
Throughout the twilight years.

Graham K Barnes

TIME

Time which separates us from all love
Are you pure vision or a concrete form
Mirrored in the lake of disillusionment
How intangible you seem

The painless bliss of solitude
All but eradicates the passion from my heart
Yet half forgotten kisses burn and sting
As clear as actuality

In continuity the seasons live
The what we were is what we are
The love we will give is the love we gave
Long years ago when we were born.

Dorothy Gibbard

UNTITLED

Calm teachings between trees in the night
Pockets of warmth and gentleness
Sigh evenly all around.
Dwelling place swept by rain
Fallen to revive again
Outbursts coloured by magic
Dance beside streams.

Animals lost to the dawn
Disconnected by words
Thoughts
And greed.

Life is a succession of choices.

Underlay. Mexican Wagon.
Stationary in the yard.
Women and words. Thoughts and pleasure.
Beds of grass, harsh and soft
Waiting for a new expanse.

Red beams.
(A silence ensues)
Darkened arena comes to life.
Fatal. Never the same again.

Christopher Kelly

ROUTINE REVIEW

Walking along the familiar passage, nothing abnormal, a routine review

Opening the door, the voices stop suddenly, strange awkward moment, a sinister hue.

Faces that normally smile in a greeting, strain to compose an expression serene

Asked to sit down while papers are shuffled, this has become an alarming scene.

A large desk divides me from three seated figures, confident, empowered, and in total control

They speak in rotation as though they were reading, from a well defined script, in a well-rehearsed role.

Words, just like rocks crashing down all around me, noise in my head, such a thunderous roar

Redundant, streamlining, market forces, re-structuring, the meaning quite clear, I am needed, no more.

Unable to grasp any reason or meaning, my senses impaired with this shock and alarm,

I sit, and I give the impression of listening, to these three seated figures, who have done me this harm.

Confusion surrounds me, unable to focus, I fumble with papers they issue and mark,

The interview ends, then they wish me success, in whatever career, I intend to embark.

Guided by instinct, I am leaving the building, my existence wiped out, no status or claim

Hushed voices of colleagues, embarrassed and frightened, unwilling, unable, to share in my pain.

Standing outside with no job or no prospects, my corporate life, it has all been a waste,

There is no reward for loyal dedication, when your name is on their list, you're removed, with all haste.

Margaret Rowland

EVERYBODY HAPPY?

A happy day at the Sunshine Club,
All the old bodies are here,
There's Mister Clegg with the wooden leg,
And Mrs Dwyer, such a Dear,
Put Mrs Moore by the loo door,
You'll not have so far to run,
She shit her knickers twice last week,
And cleaning up's no fun,
Well Mrs Paget's quite on form,
I'm sure I heard her say hello,
No Mrs Shere there are no Germans here,
Mr Rumbellow will have to go.

A happy day at the Sunshine Club.
See them all sitting round the wall,
Sipping tea and dribbling,
Wrapped in memories and a shawl.

Round them up in the happy bus,
Prise them from their shells,
Rows of naked wrinkled winkles,
Ex 1920's bathing belles.

It's a happy day at the Sunshine Club,
And membership is free,
You just need to be forgotten,
And the death side of seventy.

Stephen Briggs

1ST ON SCHOOL SPORTS DAY

The starter's gun goes off - *Bang.*
Out in front streaks Donna Lang
The shield is first in Donna's mind
While poor Naomi lags behind.
To the rest of the world Naomi shuts her mind.
She knows she's laggin' well behind
She concentrates on an even pace.
Who knows she might come in 2nd place.
Naomi keeps her small mind closed and shut
Now she's past the caretaker's hut.
Out along by the Burn
And to the bridge a left turn
Along the road around the ling
Naomi's legs begin to sting
Now along past the Gun and Crow
Naomi's not far to go.
Naomi's heart pounds in her chest
She feels the damp sweat on her vest
Naomi runs with all her might
But no-one else is in her sight
Naomi thinks they've all done fine
As she spies the winning line.
The thought 'they're fast' comes to Naomi's mind.
For me to be so far behind.
Her throat and mouth are parched and dry
Naomi thinks she's going to die.
Naomi crosses the line quite fast
only to be told *Your-Eh-First.*

Rebecca Heaslip-Armstrong

TEAR SEASON

Paint my thoughts for you in desolate landscapes
Or write these words for you whilst suffering heartaches

Destroy my hopes with fire and piercing venom
Drowning my love in an ocean's fathom

When summer sun be darkened from clouds
Then bury our hearts in grey silken shrouds

These silent voices that once knew passion
Now lovers and loving fall from fashion

Forgotten, forsaken, for never a reason
Now this be the start of another tear season.

Allan Bance

SEASONS

Summer - The sun is warm
So clear and bright
It is so high in the sky
Down below the people scatter,
Too warm and hot for it to matter.

Autumn - Autumn is a sign of colours,
When the leaves sprinkle down
to the ground.
They are a beautiful colour
Red, yellow, green and brown.

Winter - The frosty night covers the sky
It's winter time again.
It makes the trees
So cold and bare,
And whistles through the doors.

Abigail Campbell (13)

DOG ON A SETTEE

Dog on a settee
Just about contented
Fidgeting
From time to time
As humans interrupt
The flow of sleep

Brown eyes bleary
Against the blue
Material
Muscles aching
From the strain
Of relaxation

After an hour or two
Or three or four
The heavy body
Sighs and stretches
What's in the way
Is in the way

And fat paws
With outstretched claws
Press into human thighs
Upsetting teacups
Catching accidentally
The macramied cushions.

Philip Harris-Worthington

SPRING WAYS

A spring morn
Begins with a gold dawn,
And the sun begins to shine.
A spring night
Begins with the sun's flight
As the stars fall into line.

The blossoms begin to bloom
Before their winter doom,
And the moist spring air
Tells a flower
That a shower
Will make it the beauty of the flower fair.

But night
Falls with the starlight,
And the beginning of the flower's woe:
As a cold gale
Tells the tale
Of the coming winter snow.

The flower
Did not wake, in the cold shower
That winter had brought:
A lesson so sad,
That is, not to be too glad,
Our Holy Father has taught.

Trevor S King

SOMEWHERE WHERE I'VE NEVER BEEN BEFORE

Country walks with father were the times I loved the most,
Climbing misty mountains or hiking on the coast.
But not for me the old haunts - I wanted to explore.
'Take me somewhere Daddy, where I've never been before.'

On Sundays when we left our home and started on our way,
my family would laugh at me each time they heard me say -
'Take me somewhere Daddy where I've never been before.
Let's go down another lane and to a different shore.'

As I grew up I met the man who was to share my life,
bringing me such happiness and halving all the strife.
'Let us face together what life may have in store -
Take me somewhere darling, where I've never been before.'

Then one windy night as our baby stirred inside,
He was proud to drive me on a very special ride.
We faced the birth together with joy and fear so raw.
He took me somewhere different, where I'd never been before.

At last our child was born, and soon there came two more.
'Take us somewhere Daddy where we've never been before.'
Once more we tramped the moorland and scrambled to the beach,
or sometimes climbed a distant peak that seemed beyond our reach.

We often talked of father and how he showed the way
by taking me on country walks in my happy childhood day.
But father's health is failing now and he can only dream
of how we chased the distant views which aren't quite what they seem.

He cannot walk the garden path, his legs so weak and frail.
He knows he'll no more seek to hike a dusty mountain trail.
Perhaps he's nearly ready, at four score years and more,
for God to lead him somewhere where he's never been before.

Brenda Gates

SUMMER

Thistledown that dips and peaks
blown in summer's golden cheeks
Fragile ball adrift on high
silver motes in blue, blue sky
Wayward elfin spirit thine
no fairy hand can thee confine
Glinting light and joyous tossed
bright as hope - a moment, lost!

P J Kyle

THE OVERCOAT

I close my eyes
In the darkness I cannot see
And then I can pretend no-one else can.
I can fool myself that all is fine
That the clouds still pass me by
And the waves still crash the shore.
Pulling on that heavy overcoat
They call oblivion
I wear it with guilt
But it is better than tears.

I am guilty for the lies,
But that I can hide in my inside pocket.
It is the salty burning behind the guilt
Preventing the coat from fastening
Forcing it upon everyone
When all I want to do is hide away.
When I was a child
I was afraid of the darkness,
Now it is welcomed in my wardrobe
Waiting to be slipped into.

Karen Allen

MARY'S LOVE

Mary smiled. With joy she knew
The baby which inside her grew,
Would be the Son of God - His plan
To come to earth himself, as man.

Mary sang. She went away
And with Elizabeth did stay.
They shared their news. God's Spirit came,
Their lives would never be the same.

Mary sighed. Her babe was here,
In stable room so crude and bare.
Such love was in the manger there -
A love for all mankind to share.

Mary searched. Her son to find -
Where had he gone? She had in mind
A childish prank. She might have known
In His Father's house he was at home.

Mary watched. Where was her son
Who left his home, work to be done?
There, people did not want to know
The message He was sent to show.

Mary wept. Here was her son
Upon a cross for sins we've done.
How great her pain! Yet she stood by
As they her Son did crucify.

Mary laughed. Her grief had gone.
Her Son, no longer in the tomb.
Alive - she knew this was God's will,
The role of Saviour He would now fulfil.

Elizabeth Ruse

THE FOX

The fox, is an animal
with fur like the
Burnished Sun
his nose is
sharp and pointed
with eyes so tiny

He stealthily creeps
into the farmyard
at the dead of night
and creeps like a shadow
to the hen-house
on four silent feet

So quietly he went
they never heard him
he snatched at the
biggest fattest hen
and killed her dead
with teeth so sharp

Then with the farmer asleep
unaware of the danger
off into the night
he silently vanishes
with fur like the
Burnished Sun.

Laurence Sutherland

UNTITLED

That day we met just by chance
Your half closed eyes, that backward glance
The surging feeling as you stood near
The thrill I felt yet the silent fear
That you may guess my wildest dreams
My love for you and all that it means
I smile and look, then walk away
Hoping that perhaps one day
You may by chance just think of me
And wonder how our love would be

Think of me sometimes
Now you are gone
Wonder about me
And how I am going on
For I will be thinking of you every day
Of the times we spent together
And the things you used to say
Like how I was so special with
a love that was new
Something you had never known
The love I gave to you
your feelings changed towards me
But my feelings stayed the same
To me you meant everything
To you it was just a game
So think of me sometimes
If only with a smile
Keep me in your memory
If only for a while.

Veronica Taylor

MY SPECIAL FRIEND

This friend is such a special chap,
with comforting expression,
he'll listen to your problems,
and clear your mental vision.

He's brave! He's warm! He's loving too!
He'll never answer back,
he's never ever angry,
he's such a placid chap.

You can always count upon this friend,
his friendship is so steady.
Who is it that I talk about?
The ever faithful *Teddy!*

K M Edmondson

IMPRESSIONS OF BLACKPOOL

We sit on the prom in the hazy sun
like thousands before us have already done.
We stare at the beach
and the grey sea beyond
and hear in the background
the tatty pigeons' song.
The man with the chips
now sitting close by
has already caught the herring gull's eye,
Here they all come, where are they from
as they swoop on by patrolling their prom
and the donkey man sits there still
on his wooden chair,
Waiting in vain for one more fare.

S Markham

HEART

Two hearts,
Open as one -

Sky so blue,
Also cool

Two silver moons
With a pink and yellow
Mist surrounding them

In, and around space are the
futile beginnings of man, and
a spaceship called
Voyager -

Thirty years, or more man set
foot on the moon, in which
hearts collide

Earth, so far away
not like space
So blue -

And holding, life
so new -

Mark Lloyd

SUNDOWN

The sun dips slowly out of sight
And heralds the approaching night
The air feels cold, the sky turns blue
And slowly darkness creeps anew

The darkness wraps around the towns,
The cities, dulling sights and sounds
All is quiet, all serene
Everything becomes a dream.

Suzanne Gifford

ANGEL OF LOVE

She fell from the sky, and there she was
An absence so serene, so loving, so beautiful.
I wrapped my arms around her, engulfed her in my love,
It was so divine. My heart expanded to trap her within.

No book of knowledge can unravel the dark mystery of my soul.

The light shone bright, the cloud lifted and there I stood
Naked as the day I was born.
'Welcome little one, welcome to reality
You are me I am you, we are all one.'

The tears fell
The love so great, the experience so beautiful
Engulfing all of me - Body and soul
My heart expanded to take all that was given.
'Don't be afraid little one, you are loved so complete
We are with you always - Don't ever forget
We will survive all of us, the beauty and love is all
All is one, one is all.
You will feel lost at times
We are here, surrounding you with a love so divine
No anger, no pain, no hurt.'

Rosemary Reader

LIFE STILL GOES ON

The burnished leaves blithely flutter from the trees,
Upon the ground so stealthily they lie,
Each one a dream not realised,
As years slip swiftly by.

Greg still comes in with muddy knees,
Wants tea, and help with homework please;
Now! Where's the little scoundrel gone?
Oh! Yes my dear, life still goes on.

Old Tabby, Tibby died last year;
We buried her beneath the pier,
Where she loved to laze in languid splendour;
With serenely not a care.

Last spring we filled the fish pond in;
Now flowers resplendent grow so tall;
The scent of stocks pervade the air;
Their shadows crouch against the wall.

Night now descends in velvet cloak,
The breeze blows softly, now contrite,
The clock tick on relentlessly,
And so my dear, goodnight!

P Cowley

THANKFULNESS

Walking my dogs every day,
Along the river we like to play.
If I'm feel very sad
I think of these things and I feel glad.

Look at the wildlife and the trees,
See the flowers and the bees.
God made them all, also the river.
He is the taker, and He is the giver.

For when I have been near death's door
It makes life more precious, than ever before.
I can be busy like a beehive,
And very thankful to be alive.

As we head home to our abode.
I feel as if I've shed my load.
Thanks to God for my health.
With things like these, who needs wealth.

J Vokes

THE SOUND OF SILENCE

Loneliness called me from the shadows
'Speak to me, pretend,
you have joined the land of solo
and I shall be your friend'
The voice caressed my silent world
the solitude that was my home,
But the rules of solitaire were broken
for I was no-longer alone.

With the luxury of conversation
I clutched at every word,
But bid the voice to speak in whispers
lest we be overheard.
The voice cried out in laughter,
'Are you blind to the truth, can't you see?
'If there were anyone who cared for you
then you wouldn't be talking to me!'

The truth of these words pulled at my heart
and I dragged myself out of my chair
I walked to the voice, deep into the shadows
but found there was nobody there.

K V Lillico

THOUGHTS OF A TORTURED WOMAN

The doctors say I'm going mad,
That deep inside I'm very bad.
I killed my father,
My mother too,
Because I gave my love to you.
My father had a heart attack,
When to my house I brought you back.
My mother might as well be dead
She's too far gone inside her head.
You made me think that I was dirt,
For you to walk on, for you to hurt.
I never thought you'd let me be,
For you were evil right through you see.
My innocence just walked away,
When across my path you did stray.
Now I'm here and going mad,
Because I killed you,
I'm not sad.

Sarah Bennett

THE KISS

I close my eyes, your hand in mine
I hear your voice, its warm caress
I feel your touch, it's so devine
Our bodies lay entwined
Your soft sweet lips pressed up
to mine.
Please do it once more, it feels
so fine.

Heidi Chalfont

SOLDIERING

You'll feed on beans and rotten hay,
A horse's hoof come your naming day,
You'll sweat and bleed 'til you grow old,
And your only gold, will be dreams of gold.
If you go to be a soldier,
If you go to be a soldier.

Your girl will marry another man,
A muddy grave will be all your land,
Food for the worms and none to mourn,
You'll curse the day you were ever born.
If you go to be a soldier,
If you go to be a soldier.

Dale Mullock

ESCAPE

She's trapped inside an impenetrable cage,
A cage of her thoughts and emotions.
A collapsed world is inside her head,
It stops her from running away.
She tries to break through,
She tries to break free,
From the bars of her conscience and fears.
When she's almost there she is knocked down again,
By a wave created from tears.
Can anyone hear her cries of despair?
If they could, would they care?
Would they take her by the hand,
Help her try to make a stand?
Build up the world that has fallen around her,
Instead of the tears help her join in the laughter.
Show her there's someone who understands,
The struggle to escape her mind.

Louise Tighe

YOU DON'T SEE ME

You don't see me, do you?
I could be a million miles away
And it's prompted me to say
What I feel.

You don't see me, do you?
The little dreams I dream
And the comfort that they seem
Just aren't real.

You could look me in the eye,
You could smile at me, laugh with me,
You wonder why I sigh,
You don't see me . . .
Do you?

You don't see me, do you?
I'm just a face upon the street
Just someone who you meet
From time to time.

You don't see me, do you?
You don't see the tears I hide
Or the pain I hold inside
'Cause you're not mine.

If I seem a little shy
I'm afraid of looking foolish,
But it wouldn't matter, why?
You don't see me!
Do You.

L C Evans

GOING UNDERGROUND

You're getting older, greyer by the day,
You're withering away, yes you've had your say,
You'll soon be meeting your maker,
But first stop it's the undertaker.

Now there's no doubt,
Your candle has blown out,
With one final gust,
You were gone with the wind.

Your hair will fall out,
Your teeth will drop out,
No more a-roaming,
This is where you must stay.

Christine Lee

CASTLES IN THE SKY

If one has dreams they have the world
At any time of day
They're worth all the treasures in the land
And should not be thrown away

A brand new car
A horse with grace
A solid oak table with Nottingham lace
To own a house right by the sea
Or a cottage in the country.

In my mind's eye, I have much more
But all these things I keep instore
For all my dreams that reach so high
To build my castles in the sky.

J Blenkinsopp

BERLIN NIGHT BAR

Our coats all damp with drizzle
Huddled in the opiate
Dark red glow of recklessness
That is the Domino Bar

Badger Piers for four more beers
Ceremoniously
We pass the nightly pipe around
Smoke fills the Domino Bar

Crawling decadent darkness
Like wolves at the store room door
We howl and snort and then howl
again in the Domino Bar

Eric casting runes of sex
Leather and perversity
Gyrates his hips to Hendrix
Down in the Domino Bar

Fabio bitches at Piers
You content in your chair
PJ and I all howled out
Depart the Domino Bar.

Teresa Evans

ANGEL IN ASPHALT

I can move concrete under foot
asphalt scent like incense
and I'm breaking
I move with the four winds
glide and touch the sun
I lay down in heat on the riverbed
and harden like the scum

I'm a high plains drifter
walk the edge of the plateau
and if a crack, should appear
I'll break my bones for you
        I'm breaking
sucking in the ocean
It's filling in my chest
lay with me on the riverbed
where we'll take our rest.

S Y Wilson

FRIENDSHIP

Never give up on the love of a friend
no matter how the picture is painted.
Doubt does not belong, neither does rejection,
true friendship is not for the faint-hearted.
Value a friend with trust and an open mind,
never look too long at the flaws,
for love must rise above all of these.
Though sometimes hurt is caused
by misunderstandings, a thoughtless deed,
remember of all things you may ever hold
friendship is one of the most precious.
So once having found it, with wonder enfold
and you will never be alone if you can give
this gift of love to someone in your life.
The joy of knowing that you have found
another who can love you in return
then despite all the wrongs in the world,
the empty days and darkened nights
known to everyone
will become full and bright
with the love of a friend.

Caroline Nash

EMILY

Oh beautiful lady would you come to my bed,
And lay yourself beside me while I sleep
Would you listen to my heartbeat,
Through the silence of my dreams,
In the quiet of my surroundings,
In the company of my queen.

Our bodies could lay together in love,
With tender touches warm,
From the heat of passion comes,
Tranquillity and calm.

One look, one smile, one friendly word,
Spoken from the heart.
Just one kiss from your sweet lips
And a thousand dreams may start

I will wait and till you come,
I will lay alone,
And if you come I will repay,
The love that you have shown

And through the darkness,
Where I lay,
Your eyes will clearly see,
A love so strong within my heart,
My love for
Emily.

Mark Himlin

TWELFTH OF MAY

Twelfth of May, evil day
That's the day you were taken away
No more to wake, no more to laugh
Lady of mine, now that's all past.
Touch of your body, grip of your hand
Now all lost to a new promised land.
Walking in gardens, strolling in places
All gone forever, oh, how it creases
Me up to believe I never again
Shall be in your presence, just as and when.
Sleeping in aircraft, high in the skies
Dozing in deckchairs, closing your eyes.
Waking and laughing, tired or bright,
Stealing a kiss, morning, noon or night.
And in the Marsden, all of us together
Laughing and joking, hoping that never
The end would come, and we would part
Each moment was magic, shared from the heart.
Singing together with memories long gone
Our anniversary, our own special song.
Saying 'I love you' and 'I love you too'
For the millionth time, or was it two?
Like a blow from a hammer, my one special friend
On Friday our together came to an end.
I wept when we were parted on that fateful day
To a glorious sunset you were spirited away
Never to return, you flew like a dove
To share with others the depths of your love.
Twelfth of May, sadness day
That's the day you were stolen away.

Mike Jackson

AUTUMN TREE

Oh how beautiful you stand so tall,
Blowing in the wind when autumn falls,
Leaves from green, yellow, then brown,
Dropping in the wind from time to time,
And when your leaves have all gone, you stand so bare,
Ready for the battle ahead,
Oh, how bare you look, when just a stub,
Waiting for the winter months to come,
Oh how beautiful you stand,
Blowing in the wind when autumn falls,
It's not the seasons that you fear,
It's not the gales or storms that you will feel and hear,
But mankind with their ideas,
The saws or choppers, from time to time,
Will you survive another year, oh how you must fear
Nature's cruel and nature's kind,
But the biggest threat to the tree is mankind,
Open your eyes and you will see, the beauty of a tree,
Oh how beautiful you stand, blowing in the wind
When autumn falls.

N Adair

ADAS

I am here, you are there,
You are here, there I am.
There you are, here I am,
Lies the crisis of the modern man.

We share the same air,
We share the same sky,
We awake by the same light,
The same moon that guides us,
At night

How can I continue to live,
How can my heart continue
to beat?
When you have the other half,
Give it me back, as you only live
across the street

I don't understand
I'll never know why,
We don't share the same feelings
But yet, we've shared the same
piece of sky.

Andrea E Cope

BLACK AND WHITE

Black and white.
Blackness and whiteness.
Yearning for simplicity and certainty
amid the frothing torrents of our threatening world.
Permanent castaways from the happy utopias we'd emigrated to,
Our pallid lives imperfect scrub marks in the onward rush
To the ultra-comfort zones of brochure paradise.
Had we time,
If we realised that we had time,
We might notice the panic stricken faces of friends and strangers
Are not reflections of a heaven on earth that awaits
But pain leaking through the holes in our soul.
There is no end while we travel onwards.

Alun Morris

NEARLY THERE

The night sounds of the ward kept him awake,
The coughing, spluttering, and clanging
That were the usual accompaniment to the
Pall of pain and sickness that hovered over all.

Some bright lights came on; a nearby patient
Was being treated by the red-headed nurse.
Another bed was being put into an empty space
As a patient from surgery was wheeled in.

Slowly and imperceptibly, the bright lights
Seemed dimmer; the sounds of the hospital night
Retreated, and he became aware that a feeling
Of lassitude and comfort eased his painful
Body, as if a balm had been given at last.

His mind became a blank, and he began to drift
Into a better world where there was no pain.
But, suddenly, it all changed. Faces close to
Him shouted at him, calling him back from the
Release that was almost his.

Reluctantly, he joined life again, and the pain
Flooded back, somehow intensified by being
Missing for some time. All around him was the
Usual frantic bustle of a dying man being revived.

As he slowly came back to life, he knew a secret.
That death was an easement, a relief, and
Should not be feared. Somehow, his acceptance
Of that fact brought the comfort he needed.

Alex McClure

DESTRUCTION

Standing stark against an autumn sky
we have watched the seasons change her
my love and I
solemnly she dances
to the tune of the whistling breeze
stripped of all her glory
bare of all her leaves

the orange tape around her seals her fate
the morning will bring men
with grim faces to our gate
once their path is clear
no trees stand in the way
will our land be flattened
by the end of another day

will then they pave it over
to make way for many cars
will the air be safe to breathe
now the earth is marred
I say a silent prayer
remembering how she was
I hope my prayer is answered
it will be if there's a God

if there's any justice in the land
where chaos seems to reign
then maybe we can heal the earth
of all the needless pain

Sally Spelling

A PEN FULL OF DREAMS

If I ruled the world, we'd not be born young, but old!
The wrinkles we have, would get less, fade and unfold.

Our thinning white hair would grow longer and thicker -
And on our keyboard, we'd get quicker and quicker.

Our glasses and dentures would become yesterday things -
And, as for our feet, well, they'd simply grow wings.

We'd bloom and blossom until we were young again -
You'd be amazed by the schemes dreamed up by my pen.

We'd go to the Big Market on a Friday night -
Wearing a mini, of course, not a coat in sight.

Then back to school we'd go, and start at the top,
And get smaller and walk with a jump, skip and hop.

As an infant babe, I'd get fed on demand -
If I didn't get my way, I'd play the band.

But, alas, I'm not God, so grow old I must,
And p'raps, like a vintage car, I'll not show the rust!

Pat Berkshire

FREE

Wolf stands alone upon the top
Of a mountain way up high.
The night is dark, the moon is bright,
You can see him if you try.

The Indian roams throughout the land,
He carries his home around.
He sets up camp and cooks his tea,
And he sleeps upon the ground.

The spirit world is all around;
You cannot see, but you feel
Their presence as it flickers by
On life's continuous wheel.

The Indian and wolf are free;
Their spirits both are flying.
They soar upon the gentle breeze
To comfort when we're dying.

S Leak

WHO AM I?

Who am I?
I just can't say
My life is a lie
The truth went astray

When all my turmoil
Bursts at the seams
Then I recoil
Into my dreams

I couldn't care less
What they think of me
I might be a mess
But my love is free

You ask me to act
In a different way
But it's a fact
That soon I'd stray

Back to the me
I've always been
But not the me
That all have seen.

D Carr

METAL MANIA

Why is it that you work for him
You never seem to stop,
Yet you look at me and on a whim
Disaster's all I cop!

You laugh at me, I know you do,
You wait for my return.
You see me come, you go askew,
You fuse, you flood, you burn.

When he's around you're meek and mild,
You work without a hitch.
When I arrive I feel beguiled,
Until the sudden glitch.

What is it that you see in me,
To make you act this way?
I do not work you endlessly,
You do not toil all day.

Yet once I've turned the switch to 'on'
You seem to go berserk.
You glower at me, all pretence gone,
And then refuse to work.

I'd dispose of you if I only could,
You're cruel, unkind and mean,
You terrify, you're just no good,
You monstrous washing machine!

Susan Sugden

TRUE LOVE OR BLACKMAIL?

Love me forever
Or not at all,
I couldn't take it
If you didn't call,
Didn't phone,
Just to say
Hey,
How's it going?
You'd be showing
That you cared.

All we've shared
Counts for something.
Doesn't it?
Shouldn't it?

Like Juliet and Romeo
I know
That if you leave,
I'd grieve,
I couldn't cope;
I'd have no hope
Of coming to terms
With it.
I'd rather die.
So is this goodbye?

Stephanie J Davidson

I WAS AWARE

Does no God hear when I pray?
When I see the interminable grey
skyline of this bland bleak day.

When I grasp a grey figure in bed,
her fragility races 'round my head,
that next week she might be dead.

Criminal for me to anticipate
death, for me to formulate
these ideas, to even contemplate

the agony, the pain, the tears.
They will jostle for space, spear
through the hopelessness, rear

perhaps one welcome gleam of peace
that can only be termed as release,
if we don't have to deal with the grief.

I feel safe now as she may too.
A guiding force will ensure her through.
Now, she wanders to the back of the queue.

Rebecca Jones

SNUGGLES

Snuggles is my kitten,
She is black and white.
She comes in for her dinner,
And then stays out all night.
When I ask her where she's been,
She gives a little meow -
And looks at me as if to say
'That would be telling now!'

Lebony Herbert (10)

DAWN

From my pillow the honey coloured dawn rises
Rising to the cobbled blue skies above
Below, the river Fal like a millpond on the sea
With the mist rising obscuring the landscape
The trees stand proud above the mist
Like soldiers guarding the sea
The wake of the Flushing ferry
Carves through the still river
To collect the children in time for school
The yachts at their moorings stand like sentinels
Awaiting a breeze on a calm sea
It is morning now and all the mist has gone
The fields are bathed in morning sunlight
Cattle tread the morning dew
Munching the new green grass
Eight swans glide by for breakfast at Penryn
And curlews are drying their wings on a yellow dinghy
The pleasure boats leave their moorings
To show the people the wonders of the rivers
An aircraft glides over the cobbled sky
Its path an unknown destination
The docks start their morning work
On ships from distant lands
I search my mind
Who built this wonderful world of ours.

A W Holden

BOYS!

Bruised legs
Scratched face
Broken arm set in plaster
It seems to me, the boys live their lives
Going from disaster to disaster

A mother seems to worry
Throughout his waking hour
He will fall in ponds and play with mud
But never take a shower

He seems to have an allergy
To water and to soap
The intake of food is never ending
How does his stomach cope?

He sits for hours in his bedroom
Playing music much to loud
His friends leave much to be desired
He always likes the wrong crowd

But then he notices another world
Of females, all sweet like honey
But he can never take them out
He is always short of money

Until that day that he brings her home
The girl that's to be his wife
And you must come to terms with it
He is about to start a new life.

Erica M Harnett

TIME WITHIN

Within the walls which surround the city,
time cannot stand still,
though tourists come throughout the year,
they do so at their will

The hustle and bustle of shoppers,
and business men from afar,
bus companies competing,
and the congestion of the car.

Outcasts taking drinks or drugs,
and sometimes even glue,
in car parks or on benches,
and street corners too.

The Town crier stands in the 'centre',
ringing out upon his bell,
'Oh yea!' 'Oh yea!' he's shouting,
then from his scroll he'll tell,
of places which surround us,
and events for all to try,
bringing joy and laughter within the echo
of his cry.

Upon the 'Walls' of Chester,
historic views to see,
a towering Cathedral with gardens,
a relaxing place to be.
Where upon the lawns of beauty,
you collect a precious thought,
. . . somewhere within the walls of this city,
times are often caught.

W Aisthorpe

TOYSHOP WINDOW

When midnight strikes they come to life
Toyshop belongs to man and wife.
In the window sitting there
Move in the day, they wouldn't dare,
Now they are to have some fun
When shops are closed and day is done
Clockwork toys start to dance,
Dolls and teddies preen and prance,
Trains go round the track at speed
Monkeys on bananas feed.
As dawn comes up, all is calm,
It didn't really do them harm,
'Hope none of us is sold today,
let's get the next party under way!'

Brenda Elvery

MY EVERYTHING

You are my everything.
My life my all
You are the ocean deep
The mountain tall
You are the morning light
My sunny day
And there is never a night goes by
That I couldn't say
You are my star above
The moon on high
If I should lose your love
My heart would surely die
I know that I'll be yours
Till heaven above should fall
For you're my everything
My life, my love, my all.

James Anderson

SPEED

They all think I'm too young,
And that I don't understand.
But I'm old enough to know
That life doesn't go as planned.

She was my best ever friend,
When I needed her she was there.
At first everyone was sympathetic
But now no-one seems to care.

I remember her face;
Her eyes and her smile.
The way she used to laugh
The way she cried once in a while.

We did almost everything together,
She was the sister I never had.
I shared her joy when she was happy,
I shared her sorrow when she was sad.

But I couldn't share her hurt,
When she was thrown to the ground.
By the car that went too fast
And didn't even wait around.

People think I should have warned her,
About the car she didn't see.
But she ran into the road so fast
Now she's just a memory.

I'm still hurting inside,
I don't know when the tears will end.
But do the drivers cry too,
When they speed and kill your best friend?

Lisa Atkinson

NEVER TAKE YOUR ORANGE ON THE BUS

Ever tried eating an orange on the bus
elegantly peeling it with the minimum of fuss

As you pierce through the skin
with gentlest of ease

The juice squirts up your nose
making you sneeze

With orange in hand, juice running up your sleeve
you fumble for a tissue, your nose to relieve

You mop yourself down, then start again
to attack at the orange, without causing it pain

Gently holding the orange away from your dress
you look up to find the fat man's neck in a mess

Yes that awful moment when you pierced through the skin
juice not only hit you, it also hit him

Then just as the man gives a loud angry cough
you put down your orange and quickly get off.

Caroline Perry

MY LIFE

My life today is so unfair
The hate I see, is in his eyes
My house is not, my home anymore
He is always telling me, to get out that door

Leave us today and
Just go away
What can I do
Where can I go

So I stay inside this house of his
My children, my children
I love them so much
Not even the hate, I see in his eyes
Will drive me away
Because of my children
I will always stay.
Always.

Melba Pereira

ONGOING BATTLE

The cool woodland breeze blew across the fen,
Murdering the coldness of the hated winter frost,
Bringing the awaited warmth of spring.
It bounced and bounded, boinged and sprung,
Its childlike freedom breathing new life into the old wood.
Cavorting and rolling, screaming and shouting,
It yelled its message of warmth to the world.
Running and leaping, jumping and hopping,
It threw its message at the cold, cold ground,
Streaming over the old, cold fields,
Flowing over the frozen, wet beaches,
Tickling the noses of freshly woken hibernatees.
And when it had finished its message of peace and warmth,
It rested, preparing itself for the next day,
Readying itself for the battle against winter once again.

Gavin Parkin

FLOWERS I LOVE

I love the dainty snowdrop,
And the dancing daffodil,
Sweet violets in the hedgerow,
All give me such a thrill,
Primroses, so clean and fresh
And the lovely briar rose,
The harebell on the hillside,
It's amazing how it grows,
The tall spikes of the foxglove,
The daisies at my feet,
Sweet smelling honeysuckle
To me are such a treat,
When I see the scarlet poppies,
In a field of waving corn,
I stop, and count my blessings,
And feel glad that I was born.

P E Staveley

RAIN

We English moan about the rain,
But we have never known the pain,
Of seeing our children die, through lack of it.

Under the hot white sun,
Beneath those rainless skies,
Ethiopian children die,
With flies around their eyes.

Their helpless mothers watch them,
Painfully slip away,
Oh what they'd give, I'm sure,
For just *one* rainy day.

Pauline Isherwood

GOLF

A golfer's round is never done,
Eagles and pars sink in a ton,
But a long fairway
Stretch is never undone
Faldo Woosnam and the like,
Play the Greens like riding a bike.
But woods splice off and
Golfballs bite, as golfers
Hit them like dynamite.

Stuart Manton

LAST JOURNEY

No more grazing in the sunlit pastures,
Not to gallop again through the long grass
Nor greet the children on their way to school.
What am I doing here?
Tethered in the depths of darkness.
Down in the hold of the rolling ship,
Strange noises I have never heard before.
Strange voices talking to me,
Strange hands feeding me.
How I long for my comfortable stable
Bedded down in the warm hay
And the sound of my master's voice
At the start of a new day
Will I ever see again a field of ripening grain
Or have I grown too old to be of use again.

M Bracken

SILENCE

Silence is when you hear each thought
Silence is when all sound is nought
Silence is broken by a single sound
When silence is near, it's all around
Silence is quiet, peaceful and smooth
Silence can show more than words can in love
Silence is a smile between you and a friend
And death is a silence never to end.

Jane Fryer

SMELLY FEET

I was happily lying last night in my bed
When a strange whiff began to circle my head
The smell was intense, it bought tears to my eyes
I think it would even give a skunk a surprise
The stench it came from the other side of my room
And out of my trainers came a green swirling plume
The flies like vultures they began to swirl
As the tips of my toes they began to curl
I dashed out of my room trainers in hand
And next to the fish pond I was destined to stand
One swing of my arm and the trainers took flight
They must have given everything in there a terrible fright
Back up to my room I then was to travel
First over the grass then over the gravel
Then tired and fed up I climbed back into bed
Then suddenly realised it was not my trainers
But my slippers instead.

Lora Fitzgerald

HOMELESS

Seasons greetings I hear folk say,
But I won't be celebrating today,
As I sit here all alone,
In this old doorway I call home.

Once I had a home like you,
Loving parents caring too,
But I abused their love and care,
Didn't want to mix or share.

I made friends that were bad,
Only too late I learnt I'd been had.
Had a party when my parents were out,
Laughed when they threw glass and china about.

Now I'm homeless and all alone,
Nowhere to go and no home.
My so-called friends have cut me dead,
It's in the past is what they said.

So when you see me sitting in the street,
Give me a coin or a tasty treat.
This is the season of peace and goodwill,
Maybe there is hope for me still!

Elspeth Wells

THE THUNDERSTORM

The dark cold night is closing in,
Another storm is going to begin.
I huddle up in my nice warm bed,
Me, myself and my cuddly Ted.

The lightning comes a-crashing down,
Clashing onto our quiet little town.
I cuddle my teddy full of fright,
Then I shut my eyes and say goodnight.

Lisa Hodgkiss (12)

OBSERVATIONS

Winter -
There is cold.
The runny nose type.
And the shiver by the fire thing.
Halloween.
When kids you've never met before are
your friends for the night.
As long as there are sweets.
Bang, bang.
Oohh . . . Ahhh.
November, with its burns and fire engines.
And Christmas
Never mind when Jesus was really born.
We are merry - then more.
All your toys get broken
Winter . . . in a nut shell
Trodden into the carpet and not found until spring.

Rhoda Greaves

WAR ZONE

A little girl so far away
Stood looking down down on a grave
My brother my sister my father
You know they lay here where
no shadows go I tried to look her
straight in the eye and she cried out
why oh why penniless and starving
left all alone this is what life's like
in a war torn zone.

C Shannon

FLOWER OF THE NIGHT

Hello little flower so alone, but bright,
The morning dew is here and it will some be light
Alone in this big strange world are we,
Let us listen to the birds and believe we are free.

Come whisper your tales you know so well,
Of the hatred and killing, there are so many to tell
How do your radiant colours flow in the night
Taking the place of hatred and spite.

Little flower is that a tear you have shed,
I'm here to help you, back from the dead.
No more darkness or morning dew,
Just me little flower and you.

B McGough

WHERE ARE WE GOING

Up we get at the crack of dawn
faces looking quite forlorn,
we pack our things and off we go.
We leave the town with its houses and streets.
The road takes us out to far away places,
past fields and hedges and sheep and cows,
lots of trees and wide open spaces.
Where are we going, and what can we see?
And then the words ring out,
I can see the sea!

Marion Lee

PLACE YOUR BETS

Did you ever place a bet,
To try to clear a debt.
Have you ever been too slow,
To call house at Bingo.
Did you ever feel irrational,
Placing a bet on the national.
Have you ever been to a casino,
And watched your money go.
Did you ever play a bandit,
For the jackpot to try and land it.
Have you ever done the pools,
Or do you think it's for fools.
Did you ever buy a lottery line,
Thinking it's me this time.
Have you ever rolled the dice,
Or did you think twice.
All of the above is mere preamble,
Because, when you think of it,
Life's just one big gamble.

K Paterson

WELL DONE

The sun is shining, it's a perfect day,
Not a single cloud to be seen.
The sky is a beautiful shade of blue,
And the grass a delicious rich green.

How shall I spend my time today,
Effort and pleasure combining?
I cannot pass up a chance like this,
I must strike while the sun is shining.

I could mow the lawn, or trim the hedge.
My resolve appears to be slipping.
My mind is made up, I know what to do,
It's a fabulous day for stripping.

I carefully make preparation,
I must do everything just right,
It would be best to wear sunglasses
To protect my eyes from the light.

I've never done anything like this before
And I'm wondering if I dare.
I'll remove my top coat and all underneath,
The aim is to be stripped bare.

I decide to ignore passers by
And disregard their derision.
I am sure it's not so unusual
To encounter such a vision.

Yes, it's a super day for stripping
And I intend to do it so well.
When all the old paint's off the porch frame
The new top coat will look real swell.

Joan Jackson

A TIME TO MOURN

It isn't wrong to shed a tear
To grieve when one has gone, so dear,
A Mum, a Dad, a pet maybe,
A member of our family.

To God for life our thanks we give
He gives us all the strength to live,
But when He takes that life away
We feel such sadness on that day.

Our lives would be so meaningless
Without God's help - in such a mess,
Yet Him we blame when comes the end
Of mother, brother, sister, friend.

So if in Him we put our faith,
Why can't we accept that by His grace
He takes that loved one He has made
Away from us, for whom we've prayed.

The timeless promise He's made known
To those who love Him, those alone,
We'll be together, all who believe,
So why be sad, why should we grieve?

He made us all in human form,
Through weakness, ignorance, we mourn,
So God, please grant us through endurance
Eternal life through your blessed assurance.

Margaret D Ghori

SPOOKY!

It's all Hallows Eve,
or Halloween,
when goblins, spirits and witches are seen
at the midnight hour,
when the moon is bright,
it's a weird and eerie, spooky night.

Children playing Trick or Treat
in fancy dress,
on every street,
carry pumpkin lanterns
bright as day,
to frighten the witches and warlocks away.

One poor witch,
not frightened but sad,
although she's been extremely bad,
cannot fly to the witches' ball
for her broomstick always
seems to stall.

Some say she's not a witch at all!

She doesn't cackle and hasn't a notion
of how to work spells
or mix a potion,
she has a dog,
but not a cat
and she's never seen a toad or bat.

So when it comes to Halloween,
this witch is very rarely seen,
preferring to watch a film for fright,
on this weird and eerie, spooky night.

Jennifer Sykes

LUCKY GUYS

I open my door, and step outside
Another new day has begun
The birds are singing
Their usual songs
The air is warm
With the morning sun
One steps onto the sidewalk
To walk way down the street
A smile, a nod, sometimes a wave
To the people
I chance to meet
I think to myself
'Ain't life sweet'
As I continue my walk
Way down the street
Then I smile, which says it all
I give a little sigh
It fills my being with so much joy
I am a lucky guy
But then we all do
At some time or other
Step through our doorways,
Yes, I guess
We are all lucky guys.

Michael W Kell

INFORMATION

We hope you have enjoyed reading this book - and that you will continue to enjoy it in the coming years.

If you like reading and writing poetry drop us a line, or give us a call, and we'll send you a free information pack.

Write to

Arrival Press Information
1-2 Wainman Road
Woodston
Peterborough
PE2 7BU